"Behold, I give you the authority to trample on serpents and scorpions, and over all the power of the enemy, and nothing shall by any means hurt you." (Luke 10:19, NKJV)

There is a great spiritual battle going on in the world! Your prayers, therefore, are needed as "compassionate warfare" against spiritual forces of wickedness. When you make the decision to become an intercessor, you become God's spiritual warrior, receiving power to fight effectively through prayer for the entire world — your family, other nations, the Church — to realize God's ultimate objective: Christ's Kingdom fully established.

Love On Its Knees offers principles that will enable you to take God's Word into your hands and employ it as a spiritual arsenal in your personal prayer life. In these pages you will come to understand intercession as not only prayer, but a way of life.

BY Dick Eastman:

The Hour that Changes the World

No Easy Road

A Celebration of Praise

The University of the Word

Living & Praying in Jesus' Name
(with Jack Hayford)

For information on the ministry of Dick Eastman write:

Every Home for Christ
P.O. Box 35930
Colorado Springs, CO 80935-3593

DICK
EASTMAN

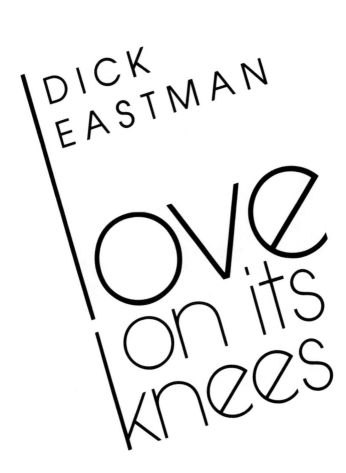

love
on its
knees

Chosen Books

A Division of Baker Book House Co
Grand Rapids, Michigan 49516

To
Jim and Joy Dawson

Jim—a unique man of God whose gentle spirit and profound administrative gifts have made possible the amplification of Joy's apostolic gifts to Christ's Body . . .

and

Joy—whom God has used mightily to impact leaders like myself in the holy and sacred art of intercessory prayer.

Acknowledgments

The heartbeat of intercession is servanthood. It is thus fitting to acknowledge those choice servants who have stood with me behind the scenes to help make *Love On Its Knees* a reality.

First, I joyously thank each of our dedicated intercessors who come regularly to our intercessory prayer room at Every Home for Christ International. Their prayer covering makes possible a continuing harvest that already has seen more than 15,500,000 decision cards come to our more than 50 global offices in the past 35 years.

To Tami Baldwin and John Sherrill I offer special appreciation. Tami's dedication as a servant is unusually exemplary. A fellow member of my home church, Tami gave countless hours, while maintaining her already rigorous work schedule, to type and retype the numerous revisions of *Love On Its Knees*, insisting she receive no remuneration.

John Sherrill, likewise, deserves special acknowledgment. One of this generation's truly gifted Christian writers, John Sherrill has set his mark on most of the pages of this manuscript. His editorial skills have helped cut through the verbiage and bring out the true heart of the message—that the fate of the world is in the hands of praying saints.

Dick Eastman
Canoga Park, California

Contents

Foreword

Only rarely do we meet those select few people who seem to incarnate their message. Dick Eastman personifies his message. In my mind, I immediately associate statesmanship in crisis with Winston Churchill, evangelism with Billy Graham. And when I think of prayer for world evangelization, I think of Dick Eastman. His passion to mobilize the Church as a prayer force for the Great Commission seems to emanate from him at every turn. I don't believe I've ever heard anyone minister who can get down into my spirit and pull at me like Dick Eastman.

It has been more than a decade now since I answered God's call on my life to seek Him in prayer. I could not conceive then of all that God would do. It is now my high privilege to assist Dick and others in calling the Body of Christ to prayer, the highest call of all. Along the way, the Lord has graced me with mentors. Dick Eastman and his Change the World School of Prayer have been a tremendous source of encouragement to me and thousands of others.

Now Dick has distilled his seasoned wisdom and offers it to you in this book. All of Dick's books are excellent but *Love On Its Knees* is perhaps his best. In these pages you will see the warm portrait of a man and his family who have made a costly commitment to prayer. You will feel the heartthrob of a man agonizing before God for his generation. You may well be challenged as never before. Most importantly, you will be given concrete steps of action to take to change the world for Jesus Christ.

As president of Every Home for Christ/World Literature Crusade, Dick seems postured as no one else to awaken the Church to the inseparable link between prevailing prayer and closure on the Great Commission. Dick is uniquely graced to cut through sectarian and denominational barriers to summon the entire Church to its most noble callings. His passion for world missions is unexcelled. His integrity is unimpeachable. And, in an age when cynicism rages out of control, his heart is unsoiled.

God has a purpose for your life. He also has a purpose for this planet. When you allow Him to fit your life into His ultimate design for humanity, then you are truly fulfilled. You will profit enormously from absorbing this book and its challenge to you. My prayer for you is that not only the didactic truths, but the heart of the man who wrote them, will by God's grace be infused into you.

> Larry Lea, Senior Pastor
> Church on the Rock
> Rockwall, Texas

one
Intercession
A Way of Life

Several years ago, in May 1986, I was preparing to take School of Prayer training to Poland at the invitation of a dynamic young pastor from Pittsburgh, Mark Geppert. Six weeks prior to my departure for Eastern Europe, I met with Mark to finalize our schedule.

"There's been a change in my itinerary," Mark said. "I'll meet you in Warsaw as planned, but first I'll be going to the Soviet Union for a month."

"The Soviet Union?" I asked, puzzled. "What will you be doing there?"

"I'm going to pray," Mark responded. "God spoke to me a few days ago and told me I was to go to Russia just to pray. He told me exactly where to go and what to pray about. I'm to pray that God will shake all of Russia. I'll ask Him to use current events—whatever they are—to shake what can be shaken, so doors will open to the Gospel and believers will have a new freedom to worship."

Thrilled that someone would go anywhere "just to pray," I asked Mark to be sure to send me a copy of his itinerary so our ministry could be praying with him before I joined him in Warsaw. The itinerary arrived and I thought little of the specifics until a few days before my departure. Suddenly, Mark's presence in the Soviet Union praying for God to shake that nation held unusual significance. Just before my departure at the end of April 1986, headlines shouted the story of a shocking incident that occurred there at a nuclear power plant in a small city named *Chernobyl*. Chernobyl, the papers said, was just a short distance from the sprawling Soviet city of Kiev. Wasn't Kiev on Mark's itinerary? In fact, if memory served me, wasn't Kiev the final place God told him to visit?

I immediately got out the letter Mark sent me listing the places God told him to visit. My recollection had been accurate. Mark's mission was to end that very weekend in Kiev with a train trip to Poland that would take him right through the area of disaster. I had been on a train trip with Mark before, in China. To Mark a train is just a long prayer meeting on tracks, moving from one place of prayer to another.

Checking the itinerary more carefully, I noted that Mark had planned to leave Kiev late on the evening of April 25, 1986, and would be passing close to Chernobyl early the next morning. That happened to be the exact time of the explosion of Chernobyl's nuclear power plant.

Only later would analysts see that Chernobyl played a major role in the events of *glasnost*, the Russian word for openness. Under normal circumstances the Soviets would have kept secret the news of such a disaster. But this was not possible with Chernobyl. In a matter of hours after the nuclear accident, scientists spotted a sudden elevation of radiation in Sweden. The source could be traced with absolute accuracy to the Soviet Ukraine.

So in the case of Chernobyl, *glasnost* was forced onto the Soviets. Being secretive was not an option. Suddenly, whether they wanted to or not, they were forced to be open.

I couldn't wait to see Mark in Warsaw. Had he kept his itinerary? If so, how had God asked him to pray?

We had hardly checked into our hotel in Warsaw before I was asking my questions. Mark indeed had kept his schedule, exactly as the Lord directed. It included four days of prayer in Kiev, ending on Friday, April 25. That day was to be the culmination of his mission of intercession. And now I was more anxious than ever to hear how God directed Mark to pray.

"Well," said Mark, settling back in his chair in our hotel room, "I went to the square in the center of Kiev and sat down under a huge statue of Lenin. Every fifteen minutes I changed the focus of my intercession for believers in Russia. I could tell when a fifteen-minute period passed because there was a gigantic clock in the square that let out a bong each quarter hour."

I asked Mark if he felt anything unusual during this prayer. "Only at the end," Mark responded. "It was on the last day, the day I made my final prayer visit to the city square. Just before noon I was suddenly convinced God had heard and that even then something was happening. Something that would shake the Soviet Union. Something God would *use* to bring more freedom."

With excitement Mark continued, "I began to lift my voice in praise, sitting there underneath the statue of the founder of Communism in Russia. But at the same time I needed a confirmation that God had heard me, so I cried out to Him: 'O God, give me a sign, even a little sign.' I waited, wondering what might happen next. And just then in the distance the hands of the huge clock moved into the twelve o'clock position."

Mark laughed as he continued, "And you know what, Brother Dick? It didn't gong. Every hour, for each of the four days I had been praying, the clock had chimed on the hour. So I waited for twelve chimes, but they never came. It was as if God was saying an old pattern was over. The very next day I began hearing about Chernobyl."

Weeks later, after reading volumes on the significance of Chernobyl, I came across fascinating information detailing events surrounding the disaster. Scientists pinpointed the first major mistake as happening twelve hours before the actual meltdown. This would have been within minutes of Mark's declaration of praise, when he knew in his spirit that events were occurring that the Lord would turn into a blessing.

Later still I heard a television commentator discussing the long-term impact of the Chernobyl disaster. "Chernobyl," he said, "means *wormwood* in the Russian language. Wouldn't it be interesting if a decade from today we were to discover that the despotic Soviet system had disappeared from the scene, replaced by a more open society, and that this change came about as the result of a simple mistake at a nuclear facility in a small Ukrainian community called . . . Chernobyl?"

It would seem that *glasnost* may be taking hold more rapidly than anyone was prepared for, opening doors where the Gospel had previously been hindered. Just two years after Chernobyl, new laws were being readied that amounted to an extraordinary retreat from power on the part of Soviet authorities. None other than Soviet Deputy Justice Minister Mikhail P. Vyshinsky said, "A revolution is taking place here. Not everyone realizes this, but that is what it is—a revolution."

And then came the big news.

At the historic General Conference of all party leaders, the first in 47 years, Soviet leader Mikhail Gorbachev made a series of statements concerning coming changes. Among them was a call for new tolerance toward the religious faiths in the Soviet Union—although, to be sure, Communism is still atheistic at its roots, and when dealing with the purported changes this should always be kept in mind.

Intercessors like Mark are rarely surprised when answers come. In fact, I'm convinced that when we stand before God with the record of spiritual successes and failures, we will learn that intercessory prayer had more to do with bringing about positive changes in our world than any other single spiritual activity.

Intercessors, in short, hold the key to releasing God's best for the world. And for the rest of this book, we will be looking at some principles of effective intercession.

These are principles that come out of thousands of hours spent in prayer over the years in a small chapel my wife, Dee, and I built in our backyard. It's just a small tool shed that we've transformed into a unique place of prayer, complete with wood paneling and extra thick carpeting. On the walls are maps and other reminders that help us pray for a lost world.

There we pray every day (well, every day when we are home) for our two daughters, Dena and Ginger; for our work, church, nation; for other nations; for our economy; for individuals in need; for ministries in need. On and on the list could go. Later we will be talking about the *discipline* of intercession. Otherwise, even prayer can become scattered and lacking in power.

The principles we will be looking at also come out of the Change the World School of Prayer, a multi-hour power training course that resulted from my call to prayer ministry almost seventeen years ago.

These two experiences—my own personal intercessory prayer life and our School of Prayer—have brought to my attention the guidelines I will be sharing in the balance of this book.

We Are the Products of Intercession

I am the product of intercession, as are all of us who know Christ as our personal Savior.

First, we are born-again followers of Jesus because our eternal Intercessor, Christ Himself, sacrificed His life on a cross as a "go-between"—or intercessor—nearly twenty centuries ago. Then, we are born-again believers because other intercessors, some not even known to us, have touched our lives over the years, breaking the demonic darkness about us that might otherwise have kept us from a full knowledge of Christ.

The primary intercessor in my life was my mother. While I was a rebellious youth involved in serious stealing and burglary by age fourteen, my mother stood against the darkness enslaving me, praying that the light of Jesus Christ would shine into my heart.

I remember in particular the day my mother's prayers seemed to catch up with me. Mike, my young partner in crime, was on the phone, asking me to go with him to our large local swimming pool.

We had developed a scheme, Mike and I, which we

carried out in the vast area where swimmers placed their towels, along with beachbags and even purses and wallets. When swimmers went into the water, we would walk casually by, select a neglected beach towel and purse or wallet, and lay our blanket on top of it. After tossing a beach ball back and forth for a few minutes, we would pick up our blanket—with the purse or wallet now underneath it—and amble innocently off.

On this particular Sunday, however, when Mike called, something came over me. I not only told him no; I told him I would never do anything like that again. I couldn't explain why. I could only tell him my life was changing.

Mike decided to go alone that day; and unknown to him a man sitting on a hillside near the pool would observe what he was doing and alert the police. Mike was arrested and taken to jail.

That night, as it was a Sunday, I went to church. God had begun to answer my mother's prayers.

Indeed, I am convinced that when we stand before God in preparation for our eternal rulership with Christ, we will discover that *every* soul ever brought to a knowledge of Christ was in some way related to intercessory prayer.

Not only is our salvation related to the power of intercession, but all that God does in and through His people is continually affected by it. Indeed, as we develop the ministry of intercession, God wants to bring to birth through us greater things than we've seen thus far.

What exactly *is* the ministry of intercession?

To Pay the Price

I am a word buff. I can easily get lost for an hour in a dictionary or concordance. Especially appealing to me are the ancient roots of a word, and I enjoy tracing how the words we use every day first came into being.

This fascination is more than just a hobby, because I find that studying the history of a word helps me to understand the concepts represented by that particular term. That's why I often take time when I'm writing about prayer to share the story of some of these words. It helps me—and, I hope, the reader—to grasp the heart of these concepts.

Intercession, for example, is derived from the two Latin words *inter* and *cedere: inter* meaning "between," "among," "involved," "intervention"; and *cedere* meaning "to go," "to yield," "to move," or "to pay the price of."

Let's look at these derivations in the order noted above.

First, the roots suggest that intercession means "to go between," as when stepping between someone and his enemy in battle. Second, these terms describe one who "yields himself" among those who are weak and need assistance.

Third, intercession is a "moving in the direction of involvement" regarding the needs and hurts of others, not unlike the generosity shown by the Good Samaritan who, as the Scripture says, "when he saw [the beaten man by the road], he had compassion on him, and went to him and bandaged his wounds . . ." (Luke 10:33–34).

Finally, intercession means "to pay the price of intervention." Christ Himself provides the most worthy example of this definition. He went to the cross to pay the price of intervention for our sins. In this regard, Christ is the supreme example of all definitions pertaining to the theme of intercession. Because He is the personification of perfection, Christ is truly the perfect "go-between."

Perhaps most essential to a well-balanced understanding of intercession is a recognition that intercession is far more a way of life than it is a type of prayer. True, intercession *is* a specific aspect of prayer, but it is much more than that. It is a style of life. Christ didn't simply engage in the ministry of intercession, for example, while He prayed for others. His very lifestyle was characterized by a *spirit* of intercession. Christ was a loving giver and His greatest gift was Himself. The Bible says He "gave His life a ransom for many" (Mark 10:45). And just as Christ's greatest gift to a lost world is Himself, our greatest gift to a lost world is our intercession. Through that intercession the world will come to know their Christ.

Foundations of Intercession

An intercessor is a man or woman—or child—who fights on behalf of others. As such, intercession is the activity that identifies us most with Christ. To be an intercessor is to be like Jesus because that is what Jesus is like. He ever lives to intercede (Hebrews 7:25; Romans 8:34)!

But where exactly do we begin our quest to become intercessors like Jesus? Four simple foundational insights assist us as we begin our journey.

First, *we must understand our "privilege" as intercessors.* Christ is ever at God's right hand, and from this position He intercedes for the saints continuously. To be at God's right hand is spoken of in the Bible as being a great privilege and pleasure: ". . . At Your right hand are pleasures forevermore" (Psalm 16:11). So when we engage in intercessory prayer, it is our privilege and pleasure to join with Christ at God's right hand in this exciting task. What could be more exciting than to be in the throne room at the heart of world-changing activity? There we are surrounded by angelic beings engaged in tireless worship as we join Jesus in destroying the works of Satan!

Truly, the work of an intercessor is a privilege at the highest level. It is to be a partner with Christ in His supreme ministry of reconciling all of humanity to God the Father.

Second, *we must understand our "position" as intercessors.* Position here, of course, doesn't concern one's physical posture as an intercessor—i.e., whether kneeling, sitting, standing, or praying prostrate—but rather to the spiritual position of being "seated" with Christ in "heavenly places." As Paul says in his letter to the Ephesian believers, God "raised us up together, and made us sit together in the heavenly places in Christ Jesus" (Ephesians 2:6).

Several interesting thoughts emerge as we consider how Christ brings us into this position.

To begin with, He *energizes* us when we are "dead." Paul says, "But God, who is rich in mercy . . . even when we were dead in trespasses, made us alive together with Christ . . ." (Ephesians 2:4–5). The Authorized Version employs the expression *He quickened us.* To "quicken" or "make alive" means to energize. It is to renew and revitalize.

Beyond this, Christ *elevates* the intercessor. Paul explains that we are "raised . . . up together." Such elevation is important in the believer's walk as it speaks of our being spiritually transported to a higher sphere of divine activity, the invisible, heavenly arena. As people who fight battles on behalf of others, we function from this elevated place, with Christ, in the heavenlies.

Finally, we are *enthroned* with Christ in intercession. We are permitted to "sit together" with Jesus beside the Father's throne, which suggests we are not merely observers of spiritual warfare but partners, involved in the administration of His divine authority.

This concept of enthroned intercessors administering spiritual authority is unusually significant. It gives us a fresh understanding of Christ's instructions to speak directly to mountains, commanding them to move (see Mark 11:22–24). When we are enthroned as intercessors we are not just asking God to do things; we are actually empowered with His authority, partners with Him as He declares His will. Bold intercessors know that God's promises empower them to operate on His behalf to command spiritual mountains to move. And it is at this level that we must understand the authority of intercessors. We are not beggars expressing personal desires but "throne room commanders," receiving orders from our Supreme Commander, Jesus, who has permitted us to use His authority in ordering strongholds to fall.

Our third foundational insight: *we must understand our "promise" as intercessors.* It is an absolute certainty that our primary objective in prayer shall be realized. That objective is to see His Kingdom fully established on earth and it is an objective established in God's Word. Isaiah plainly preached, ". . . The earth shall be full of the knowledge of the Lord as the waters cover the sea" (Isaiah 11:9).

John's Revelation describes that momentous event of Christ's Kingdom coming in its fullness as heralded by an angel who sounds with a trumpet while great shouts in heaven declare: "The kingdoms of this world have become the kingdoms of our Lord and of His Christ, and He shall reign forever and ever!" (Revelation 11:15).

One cannot escape the significance that neither this angel nor the six who precede him are permitted to sound their trumpets until first "another angel" holding a golden censer (Revelation 8:3) comes before the altar facing God's throne and with "much incense" (symbolic of worship) offers this sacrifice "with the prayers of all the saints."

John continues the description of his vision, declaring that "the smoke of the incense, with the prayers of the saints, ascended before God from the angel's hand" (Revelation 8:4).

Only then, after the prayers of all the saints are combined at the altar with the praises of God's people (symbolized by the incense), are the seven angels permitted by the Lord to begin sounding their trumpets.

Surely it is significant that all the activities that unfold are the result of the initial release of prayer mingled with "much" worship at the very throne of God (Revelation 8:1–6).

All of this serves to remind us that as intercessors we are operating under promises from God that our prayers do make a difference. Mission researchers say that some 17,000 ethnic groups are yet to be reached with the Gospel. Intercessors know their prayers will ultimately break the chains that keep these groups and people from the knowledge of Christ's love.

Finally, *we must understand our power as intercessors.* Christ called His disciples together and declared to them: "Behold, I give you the authority to trample on serpents and scorpions, and over all the power of the enemy, and nothing shall by any means hurt you" (Luke 10:19). Here we discover a dynamic promise of power most believers rarely exercise. Our Lord is saying that those who move in the direction of involvement and are willing to pay the price of intervention will have all the power necessary to confront demonic forces in their citadels.

Come with me for a closer look at this glorious ministry of compassionate warfare.

two
Compassion in Action
The Functions of Intercession

Centuries ago, during one of the darkest ages in Church history, one of a few bright lights shining was a young man named Francesco de Pietro Bernardone. Francesco was destined to become one of history's most remarkable spiritual warriors, a man who would have cities, parks, hospitals, churches, and seminaries named in his honor.

Francesco was born into wealth, the son of an Italian merchant. He seemed headed for a life of abundance in the footsteps of his father.

But all that was to change one sunny afternoon as young Francesco was riding his pony on the outskirts of the city where his father had earned his fortune. Rounding the bend along the dusty path, the pony suddenly balked, then lurched backwards. Blocking the path was a frightful sight, a leper, his limbs half eaten away, pleading for someone to help him in his final hours of suffering.

Francesco stared but a moment and then had to look away. His stomach churning, he gripped the reins tightly, ready to turn his horse back toward home.

But at that moment a strange thing happened. Francesco's eyes were suddenly opened to eternal realities. God's presence filled the youth's heart and he turned again to look at the leper. This time he did not see the infirm man; he saw himself in the man. He saw himself as God saw him, spiritually depraved. And Francesco knew that what God was seeing was a condition far worse than the dying man's leprosy.

Instantly Francesco leaped from his pony and fell to his knees beside the suffering man. He put one arm tightly around the contagious leper, while loosening a bag of gold tied to his belt with his hand yet free. Thrusting the bag into the leper's half-eaten hands, the youth bent further and gently kissed the man.

Francesco de Pietro Bernardone's life would never be the same. He surrendered to his Savior that afternoon, encountering a supernatural baptism of compassion. And this "baptism" occurred just outside the Italian city of Assisi, a city whose name would be known throughout the world for centuries to come when people spoke reverently of St. Francis of Assisi.

Channels of Compassion

Intercessory prayer begins with this same supernatural compassion; and such extraordinary caring is a gift that can come only from God. He gives it to any and all believers who will make themselves available. Because only God can give this empathy, however, we must draw near to Him to receive it. Paul told believers to "walk in love," or, as a paraphrase reads, "Be full of love" (Ephesians 5:2, TLB). Because God is love, to walk in love or "be full of love" is to be filled with God. This necessitates our spending much time in His presence to be consumed with Him.

So, compassion is at the heart of intercession. *Compassion* is derived from the two Latin words *com* and *pati, com* meaning "with" or "together" and *pati* meaning "to suffer" or "to hurt." Combined, these expressions describe one who *"suffers with"* someone in need or *"hurts together"* with those experiencing pain.

Compassion is more than mere pity. It is love in its dynamic phase, love released through action. It is a life of involvement in the struggles of others. Christ gave us the fullest expression of active compassion when He went to the cross to remove the suffering brought on humankind through sin. Jesus was not an intercessor just when He prayed, as we have already seen; He lived the life of intercession. Jesus *is* compassion. When He prayed, it was compassion praying. *To see Christ in prayer is to see Love on its knees.*

How a person lives will determine how that person prays. As Andrew Murray wrote, "It is as men live that they pray. It is the life that prays."

The fashioning of an intercessor, then, begins not so much with a burden to pray as with a burden to love—a burden that leads the intercessor ultimately to intense sessions of compassionate prayer that flow out of seven functions of intercession.

A Call to Serve

First, *intercession is serving*. It is *making oneself available*. Consider the example of Jesus, our chief Intercessor. He said, "And whoever of you desires to be first shall be slave of all. For even the Son of Man did not come to be served, but to serve, and to give His life a ransom for many" (Mark 10:44–45).

Servanthood is at the very heart of intercession. No one prays effectively for others who does not have the servant spirit of Christ. The Greek word for "serve" in Mark 10:45 is *doulos*, which means "in bondage by choice." It means to subject oneself voluntarily to the ministry of caring.

It still amazes me, looking back on the growth of our two daughters through their infant to adolescent years, that we never had to hire a babysitter. This was in spite of the fact that Dee and I made numerous missionary journeys. Such freedom was given us because a pleasant young schoolteacher, Barbara Blake, spending a pro-longed season in prayer for the Eastman family, heard God say, *I'm calling you to service in the Eastman household.* Barb had left her teaching job six months earlier to join our prayer center where college-age youths and other young single adults helped us maintain a 24-hour prayer vigil.

Shortly after, Dee and I received a call from Barb who made a stunning offer, one we were positive would last only a few weeks. Barb told us that no matter how much time was involved, nor how much notice we were able to give her, she would care for our girls while we traveled until they were old enough to care for themselves.

We decided to test the waters, so I called on Barb the evening following her offer. At first Barb simply watched the girls for a few hours while Dee and I spent some much-needed quiet moments together. That weekend there was a ministry engagement so I called Barb again. She didn't just agree to help; she agreed with unusual delight. And when we returned home Barb made us promise we would call her again no matter how short the notice. As time went on, if we didn't go anywhere for a week or two it was not unusual for Barb to call asking if we had any plans so she could guard her schedule.

Perhaps most remarkable was Barb's decision to move 350 miles south from Sacramento, California, to Los Angeles when Dee and I received the call to develop a worldwide prayer ministry through World Literature Crusade. It was Barb's idea completely, and it required finding a new job and apartment. She simply expressed her quiet view that she had made a promise and to the best of her ability wanted to keep it.

But the story doesn't end with the girls reaching their high school and college-age years. Barb still calls and still comes. She watches over our house, cat, and dog whenever the family is away. I just hope I get to stand near Barb when the "servanthood" awards are distributed around God's throne (2 Timothy 4:8)!

A Call to Fight

Second, *intercession is fighting*. It is *engaging in battle*. At first glance this seems a departure from the serving function. A spirit of fighting, however, clearly characterizes intense intercession. It is a picture portrayed best by Christ in His Gethsemane "warfare" experience (Luke 22:39–44). Because Luke is a physician, it's especially noteworthy to study the intensity of his description: "And being in agony, He prayed more earnestly. And His sweat became like great drops of blood falling down to the ground" (Luke 22:44).

The word *agony* used here by Luke comes from the Greek word *agonia*. It refers to a "place of contest" or a battlefield. Its roots are in the Greek word *agon*, which pictures a place of assembly where the Greeks celebrated their most solemn games. Unlike our modern Olympic games, however, it was not uncommon for people to fight to the death in a contest. The winner was the one who came out alive.

Praise God—Jesus came out of Gethsemane alive, victorious in a warfare so intense it could have killed Him before He ever made it to the cross. And even His death on the cross, where Christ became the living personification of intercession, was not a defeat as Satan must have believed, but a victory sealed by the miracle of the resurrection. Again, Christ emerged alive!

Paul uses this fighting theme when he requests the prayers of Roman believers: "Now I beg you, brethren, through the Lord Jesus Christ, and through the love of the Spirit, that you strive together with me in your prayers to God for me" (Romans 15:30). Here, the Greek word for "strive" is *sunagonizomai*, where the root *agonia* appears again, which is the same word translated "agony" in Luke's description of Christ's warfare in Gethsemane. Paul is saying, "While you are praying, engage in warfare against those forces that would limit my effectiveness in spreading the Gospel."

When we intercede for others we are engaging in battle on their behalf. And most interestingly, sometimes the victory we win in prayer on behalf of others actually has a way of returning to us as a blessing!

For years I have had the habit of listing in my prayer diary the names of ministers I've met. Of course, this prayer list has grown over the years, forcing an ever more prayerful selectivity in which names to add. The primary criteria were that I actually meet the person and that the Holy Spirit prompt me to add the name.

So when a Bible college student approached me at a conference asking me to add to my prayer list a friend of his who had just left for Saudi Arabia, I knew it was highly unlikely that such a thing could happen. For one thing, the friend was serving in a secular job and my policy was to put ministers only on the list. And I hadn't met the friend or his wife face-to-face. Before I could even mention my reservation the student said, "His name is George Puia, and his wife is Lynn." He spelled the name quickly and explained that although George had a secular job, his desire was to help start small prayer groups, as well as witness to Muslims as the opportunity afforded itself.

Making a mental note of the name, I added with all honesty, "My brother, I have to tell you that I can only do this if the Holy Spirit prompts me."

The student agreed that this was right. As he walked away I honestly dismissed the matter from my mind, in part because it just didn't seem that the couple fit the criteria of the list.

But two days later a strange thing happened. As I began praying for men and women on that day's prayer list, the names of George and Lynn Puia came to mind. A gentle impression came within: *I want you to add them to your list.*

Two or three years passed as I continued to pray for George and Lynn Puia. Always I wondered what they looked like, and what kind of secular work George did. Then one day I came to their names on my list and wondered if my prayers were making the slightest difference. *After all,* I thought to myself, *I haven't the foggiest idea who these people are.* It seemed to me that I was hearing in my spirit that the time had come to cease my intercession for them. With hardly a further thought I grabbed a pen and scratched their names off the list.

Several weeks later I was in Chicago, to appear on a Christian television program. Going toward the studio, I rounded a corner and ran headlong into a man hurrying in the opposite direction. I apologized, as did the brother, who looked at me carefully. Then he said, "Hey, I know you! You're Dick Eastman. You've been praying for my wife and me. I'm George Puia."

He took my elbow and ushered me gently toward the studio. "My wife, Lynn, and I just returned from Saudi Arabia, and now I'm serving as executive director for the station here."

To my amazement, the time that George and Lynn returned to the United States was around the day I scratched them from my list. Apparently the Lord wanted me to intercede for the Puias especially while they were in Saudi Arabia.

But the real encouragement to me was when George explained that our book and cassette tapes were a tool he and his wife used for starting prayer groups in that rigid Muslim land. This was interesting, since the penalties can be severe for importing such literature into countries like Saudi Arabia.

But here again, the back-up prayers of people who were interceding for George and Lynn made a practical difference. Once when clearing customs, George had a strange prompting that caused them to step back and let an Arab man behind them go first. Suddenly there was a commotion at the counter. Armed police rushed forward. The Arab man who had moved ahead of George and Lynn had been caught smuggling pornographic videocassettes, an offense that meant immediate arrest.

"Because of the commotion," George said, "the agent just motioned for Lynn and me to take our luggage and go."

A Call to Identify

Third, *intercession is identifying.* A committed intercessor often finds that involvement with others affects the very patterns of life. As Paul reminded the Corinthian believers: "Though I am free from all men, I have made myself a servant to all, that I might win the more; and to the Jews I became as a Jew, that I might win Jews; . . . to the weak I became as weak, that I might win the weak. I have become all things to all men, that I might by all means save some" (1 Corinthians 9:19–20a; 22).

Both a spirit of serving and a spirit of fighting are linked to the spirit of identification. To serve is to submit to and to assist others. To fight on behalf of others is to enter into warfare, deflecting the attacks of Satan. Such ministry clearly requires a spirit of identifying with those in need along with a willingness to adapt one's lifestyle, if necessary, in order to help meet those needs.

What does it mean to identify in intercession? It is to become increasingly sensitive to the needs of others, even to the point of denying oneself whatever is necessary to help alleviate those needs.

Intercessors, for example, learn to listen "between the

lines" wherever they go. Ordinary conversation actually becomes an unwritten prayer list for sensitive intercessors.

Learning to identify with others in prayer was an especially unique lesson God taught me over a decade ago. For days, newspaper and television reports had been filled with details regarding a hostage situation involving 153 Dutch grade school children who were being held by terrorists in Holland. The terrorists threatened to execute the children one at a time if their demands were not met.

From the day the crisis began I petitioned God to protect the children and bring about their safe release. Then a strange thing happened. Several days into the crisis the terrorists' threats intensified. That day in my backyard prayer chapel, early in the morning, an amazing thing happened. My mind was filled with a picture. But it was more than just a still picture . . . it seemed alive and I was in the middle of it. I was standing inside the schoolhouse where the 153 Dutch children were being held captive. I could see the boys and girls with my spiritual eyes. But then I saw something startling. Only 151 of the children were Dutch; the other two were our daughters, Dena and Ginger, six and nine years of age respectively.

In the natural I knew this could not be. Both the girls were fewer than a hundred feet away, fast asleep in comfortable beds. But I had forgotten that. I had slipped into the intercessor's role of identification and the Holy Spirit had ushered me into an intensity of prayer I had never before known.

Indignation swept over me and I began to command the terrorists to let the children go. I hit my fist into my palm as I prayed. I pointed my finger with authority, shaking it repeatedly at the terrorists as I demanded they release the children. I wept. I shouted. I trembled. And suddenly I sensed victory. As abruptly as the prayer had begun, it concluded.

Moments later I left my backyard prayer chapel and headed for the office. So real was the sense of victory that not another thought was given to the matter until I sat down to dinner that night with Dee and the girls. The television had been left on in the family room and out of the corner of my eye I could see the screen. I was just bringing a fork full of mashed potatoes to my mouth when the news came on. The announcer, Walter Cronkite, began with the words, "We have good news from Holland!" I froze and turned toward the screen. "We have just received word that a break has come in the hostage crisis in Holland. Three of the 153 children have been released," Cronkite continued. "It could be the beginning of the end of this terrible crisis."

My reaction surprised me. Instead of shouting a note of victory, tears came to my eyes and I returned the uneaten fork full of potatoes to my plate. My family had no idea what I was doing. *Jesus,* I said in my heart, *I didn't ask for three children, I asked for all of them to be released. And that was a prayer born of Your Spirit.*

In that instance a new burst of boldness came over me as I sharply hit the table with my fist, declaring before my startled family, "And I claim the miracle now!"

What happened next will stun me to the day I die. At the exact moment I hit the table the broadcast was interrupted by a news bulletin. Walter Cronkite was replaced by a reporter from a local CBS affiliate: "We interrupt this broadcast to bring you an update on the hostage crisis in Holland. The report given by Mr. Cronkite was recorded earlier for West Coast viewing and is incomplete. All 153 children were freed early this morning."

It was a moment of victory I will never forget. Of course, I wasn't the only believer who had prayed, but I knew my prayers had made a difference. I was especially struck by the means God used—the power of identification.

The path to intercession begins with a willingness to identify with the hurts and concerns of others. Jesus, we must remember, came from the glories of eternal beauty to "dwell among" humanity (or "pitch His tent," as the Greek word implies) so that He might pay the price of involvement (see John 1:14).

A Call to Share

Fourth, *intercession is sharing.* It is making possessions available.

In sending forth His disciples Christ issued a series of commands outlining the basics of their ministry. One simple assignment of the overall list included, "Freely you have received, freely give" (Matthew 10:8).

Sadly, many believers have yet to learn the secret of unhindered giving. They give, but not with an unreserved generosity. We note that Christ's command to His disciples went beyond mere giving. He said, "Freely give."

At the heart of meaningful intercession is the willingness to give. And often this willingness flows not out of a climate of prosperity, but conditions of poverty. In describing the churches of Macedonia, Paul says, "Though they have been going through much trouble and hard times, they have mixed their wonderful joy with their deep poverty, and the result has been an overflow of giving to others" (2 Corinthians 8:2, TLB).

Concerning this church Paul adds: "They gave not only what they could afford, but far more; and I can testify that they did it because they wanted to, and not because of nagging on my part. Best of all, they went beyond our highest hopes . . ." (verses 3, 5, TLB).

In the early days of our School of Prayer ministry there was a time when we desperately needed $5,000 to meet bills due that very day. My heart sank as I went to the post office and found only a handful of letters from our supporters. Opening the first one didn't seem to help. It contained 71 cents.

But then I read the testimony that accompanied that gift, written by a mother on behalf of her six-year-old daughter. For several years the mom had supported our ministry, sending a monthly gift that she saved out of her food budget. The previous month she had sent $20, which we had acknowledged with a thank-you note and a request for prayers concerning our payroll. And pray she did. Her prayers were overheard by her six-year-old daughter. The mother's letter told me what happened then.

"Tonight I went back into the room of our six-year-old daughter, Elisa. Elisa really loves Jesus. She asked Him into her heart when she was four. As I put her clothes away, I was startled to hear her voice. 'Mommy,' Elisa said, 'God just told me to give all the money I've saved to Dick Eastman's ministry, the man you prayed for today.' "

According to Elisa's mother, the six-year-old had tears in her eyes as she spoke, partly because the money she had saved, a grand total of 71 cents, had been carefully set aside to purchase a toy that Elisa wanted badly.

"It was a difficult thing for Elisa to give all that she had saved," the six-year-old's mother wrote, "because she really wanted that toy. But she told me she wanted to obey God even more. So, Brother Dick, enclosed is a gift of 71 cents. It's really far more than I've ever sent because even though every gift I share is a sacrifice, I've never sent all I've had."

It almost seemed as if a spirit of generosity was loosed among our supporters. When the rest of that small handful of letters were opened that morning, we had received over $8,500 in gifts—and it all began with Elisa's 71 cents.

A Call to Rule

Fifth, *intercession is ruling*. It is commanding with authority. To the prophet Jeremiah, who might be described more aptly as a "prophetic intercessor," God said: "See, I have this day set you over the nations and over the kingdoms, to root out and to pull down, to destroy and to throw down, to build and to plant" (Jeremiah 1:10).

Jeremiah was not a king or political leader. Yet he was ordained to rule over both "nations" and "kingdoms." It is significant that there are two spheres of authority— nations and kingdoms. *Kingdoms* here refer to spiritual rulers over the invisible arena, whereas *nations* refer to physical leadership over the visible arena.

Jeremiah's role as an intercessor is clearly outlined.

His calling begins with the assignment to "root out." To be an effective intercessor means going to the very source of a problem—its roots. Roots are the hidden supply source of a plant. When dealing with moral decay, roots refer to unseen forces of evil that feed the decay. Thus, Jeremiah was assigned to remove the "roots of decay" polluting their nation through intercession. To "root out" in prayer is to penetrate so deeply into a spiritual circumstance that we are able to deal directly with the primary source of that condition.

Beyond that, Jeremiah is committed to "pull down" obstacles that have been raised up in opposition to God's best for His people.

To pull down means to remove from a fixed position. The very fact that we are "pulling" something down suggests that we are removing an object that has been elevated and is fixed in that high position. Today this could refer to dictators who have been elevated to power and have become entrenched in that high position.

Jeremiah next is instructed to "destroy" these obstacles. *To destroy* means "to subdue or to defeat someone or something utterly." The intercessor is entrusted with awesome power, including the capacity to remove the influences of Satan "utterly."

There is still more. Jeremiah is commanded to "throw down" that which Satan enthrones. *Throw down* is even stronger than *pull down*. To *throw* means "to discard or remove something quickly with great force."

On my first trip to China in 1978 I often saw tables stacked high with Mao Tse-tung's *Little Red Book*, a collection of political sayings bathed in atheism. The devastating Cultural Revolution of the 1960s resulted largely from a strict allegiance to the tenets set forth in this same *Little Red Book*.

I decided to bring a copy home for use in my intercessory prayer time. I placed the small book in my backyard prayer chapel and whenever I started my intercession I was reminded to pray for China's spiritual deliverance. Day after day for over two years I would clutch the small, vinyl-covered red book in my hand, commanding it to be removed as a factor in Chinese society. My prayers were almost violent. I shouted against the influence of this book, often remembering how I had seen youth in the fields of China reading it as if they were sharing in a small group Bible study setting.

Imagine my amazement when next I visited Hong Kong to see a front page news story of Mao Tse-tung's picture being taken down—*thrown* down—throughout China. I read every word of the English language article. One paragraph leaped out with special excitement: "And as far as Mao Tse-tung's *Little Red Book* is concerned, it is as if it has disappeared from the face of the earth."

But Jeremiah's calling is not complete. Two vital responsibilities remain. What began in the negative suddenly becomes positive. Jeremiah now is told "to build" and "to plant." *To build* means to "give form to something according to a definite plan or process," or "to establish and strengthen." Intercessors must not only remove obstacles through their prayers, but they must help put something in place of what has been removed. Thus, the intercessor not only prays that an evil leader be removed; he must also pray that the right leader will be raised up.

Planting likewise is an essential ingredient to effective intercessory prayer. *To plant* means "to put something into a place where it has the capacity to grow." Intercession here rises above praying for a need. "Planting" interces- sion is involved with doing, with implementing the answers to our very own prayers. In the last chapters of this book we will see how this works out in practice.

A Call to Weep

Sixth, *intercession is weeping.* It is brokenness before God. The psalmist spoke of this aspect of sensitive intercession when he said: "Those who sow in tears shall reap in joy. He who continually goes forth weeping, bearing seed for sowing, shall doubtless come again with rejoicing, bringing his sheaves with him" (Psalm 126:5–6).

Tears that sweep over us are vitally important in victorious intercession. We see tears mentioned frequently in Scripture. There are, for example, tears of sorrow and suffering (2 Kings 20:5) and tears of joy and compassion (Genesis 33:4, John 11:35). There are tears of desperation (Esther 4:1, 3) as well as tears of travail (Isaiah 42:14) and repentance (Joel 2:12–13). Tears are pictured in Scripture as something God keeps in a bottle (Psalm 56:8), indicating that God treasures the tenderhearted.

Tears are water to the spiritual seeds we plant, thus assuring us a bountiful harvest as the result of our brokenness. More than a mere emotional garnish to our prayers, tears *become* prayers. As Charles Spurgeon explained, "Tears are liquid prayer!"

A Call to Die

Finally, *intercession is dying.* It is death to self. To Roman believers Paul wrote, "Likewise, you also, reckon yourselves to be dead indeed to sin, but alive to God in Christ Jesus our Lord" (Romans 6:11). The word translated *reckon* here means "to approach something as if." As intercessors, we are to approach each situation and circumstance

as if "dead" to all presuppositions or worldly consider-
ations. Dead means "being without feeling."

Note also the significance of the word *indeed* in the text.
Indeed means "in reality," "in truth," or "to be sure." That
is to say, we are to treat ourselves as actually being dead.
Effective intercession requires death to self. And in spiritual terms it is a real, true death—"to be sure!"

three
Intensity in Vision
The Priorities of Intercession

I am told that vultures, descending on a wounded animal, will go instantly to the eyes of their victim. It is as if they know that if any potential for life remains they must remove the vision of the victim.

Satan, like a vulture, understands the value of vision for the intercessor. Paul recognized this value, too, and prayed that the "inward eyes" of believers would be "illumined" (Ephesians 1:18, NEB).

Unfortunately, too many followers of Christ accomplish little because they lack vision. Their focus is usually scattered. A singular vision is needed. As Jack Hayford says, "When you reduce the scope of an activity or life, you increase the force of that activity or life." Water flowing through a pipe with a three-inch circumference, for example, is going to increase sharply in force if the pipe is reduced to one inch.

So it is with the intercessor who clarifies his or her vision. The Bible has much to say regarding this aspect of our instructions on intercession.

Clarity of Vision

Four foundational Scripture passages provide intercessors with a basis for developing clarity of vision.

First, Proverbs 4:23–26 helps me *determine my direction.* We read: ". . . Let your eyes look straight ahead, and your eyelids look right before you. Ponder the path of your feet, and let all your ways be established." Intercessors must know where they're going. Our eyes must focus on those issues closest to the heart of God. Who specifically has God asked me to pray for today? What nations or groups will be touched by my time with God today?

Second, Job helps me *believe in victory!* Crying out in agony, Job declared, "I will never give up so long as I live. I will not change, I will maintain the rightness of my cause" (Job 27:6, NEB).

In the midst of his intense suffering Job held securely to his belief that a sovereign God was working out something far beyond any human capacity to comprehend. True, there were times Job surely must have doubted any possibility of victory. But he refused to give up. He held onto his promises.

As believers, especially believers who intercede, we need to be tenacious. We must become fanatics who say with Job, "I will never give up." Winston Churchill once was accused of fanatacism. "I plead guilty," he said, adding his definition of *fanatic*—someone who cannot change his mind and will not change the subject. Intercessors who have a burden for a lost world, for example, have trouble keeping silent. You cannot change their minds and they will never change the subject. They've been close to the throne room so long that few other issues really matter. They have become fanatics and will not give up.

Thirdly, Philippians 3:13–14 helps me *receive my prize!* Paul speaks of "the prize" that is set before believers as being "the upward call of God." It is my opinion that no upward call is greater than intercession. Paul told the Philippians: "I do not count myself to have apprehended; but one thing I do, forgetting those things which are behind and reaching forward to those things which are ahead, I press toward the goal for the prize of the upward call of God in Christ Jesus" (Philippians 3:13–14).

To receive our prize as intercessors, Paul points to certain qualities of spirit that help us. Humility is a vital requirement. We must say with Paul, "I do not count myself to have apprehended." Singlemindedness is another requirement of effective intercession. "This one thing I do!" Paul says. A sad reality in the Church today is that so many people attempt so many things that they end up accomplishing little. And we must become good forgetters when it comes to failures. We should learn from failures but, as Paul suggests, we need to forget those things that are behind, and reach forward toward those things God has prepared for us.

Finally, 1 Corinthians 9:26 helps me *establish my goal*. Paul said, "I run with a clear goal before me" (NEB). *The*

Living Bible reads, "I run straight to the goal with purpose in every step." To the Ephesians Paul wrote: "Live life, then, with a due sense of responsibility, not as men who do not know the meaning of life but as those who do" (Ephesians 5:16–17, PHILLIPS).

Do we have clear goals? They are essential to effective intercession. Where should we look as we establish these goals? The answer, again, is to be found in our supreme example of intercession, Christ Himself. We must discover which priorities Jesus established and then pursue them with a passion.

The Priorities of the Great Intercessor

While reading the Gospel of John several years ago, I paused to meditate on the intensity of a single phrase from the lips of Jesus: "I must work the works of Him who sent Me . . ." (John 9:4). It was the expression *I must* that caught my eye. Jesus did not say, "I hope to," or, "I intend to try to." Rather, He declared forcefully, "I must."

The word *must* expresses absolute determination to carry out a task. *Must* when used as a verb, for example, suggests insistence or a fixed resolve, as in the statements "I must eat" or "I must sleep." And when used as a noun, *must* pictures an absolute requirement or unavoidable responsibility, such as, "Eating is a must."

I wondered how many times Jesus spoke of His intercessory mission by using the word *must*. With the help of a good concordance I found that there are 83,898 words in the King James text of the Gospels; yet in describing His own purposes, Jesus used the imperative *must* only eight times. These "musts" portray specific priorities in the life of Christ. Taken together, they are invaluable to us as we try to follow His example as intercessors. They include:

One: A Commitment to Suffering

In the traditional order of the Gospels, the first recorded divine absolute of Jesus (in this case expressed in the third person) is found in the description of Mark: "And He (Christ) began to teach them that the Son of Man *must suffer many things,* and be rejected . . ." (Mark 8:31, italics added).

Although referring to Himself in the third person as "the Son of Man," it is significant that Jesus employs the absolute *must.* It is our introduction to His lifestyle as an intercessor. Christ is saying that all who would become intercessors must recognize the relationship between intercession and suffering. Our first priority as intercessors is simple:

To be like Jesus, I must make a commitment to suffering.

Jesus linked suffering with rejection. Committed intercessors are often misunderstood because of their tendency to believe things very deeply and because they often hear from God in matters of serious concern. Their intensity sometimes draws the criticism that they are "off-balance" in their Christian walk, that they are so heavenly minded they are no earthly good.

Intercessors are not exempt from physical suffering. Interestingly, the Bible actually commands us to suffer. Paul told the Corinthian believers, "Don't let schisms exist in the body . . . but when one member suffers, let all members suffer with him" (1 Corinthians 12:25–26). To the Romans, Paul declared, "Weep with those who weep" (Romans 12:15). Even when we ourselves are not hurting, we are to find those who are and hurt with them. Being commanded to suffer is especially appropriate to intercessors.

This does not mean we should inflict ourselves with physical pain, but rather to realize warfare can leave battle scars as we head for ultimate victory. Jesus enjoyed the victory of the resurrection only after the agony of Gethsemane and Calvary.

Two: A Commitment to Duty

From the first recorded words of Christ as a twelve-year-old, though listed second in the traditional biblical order of the Gospels, emerges a truth that provides us with our second priority principle of Christ (see Luke 2:48–49). As a Jewish child of twelve, Jesus was taken to Jerusalem for the ceremony commonly called the Bar-Mitzvah. He was "coming of age," and the Bar-Mitzvah was that occasion acknowledging His moving into puberty. Many family members joined in the festivities. This makes it easier to understand how, when leaving the Temple for the long journey home, the parents of Jesus thought their son was elsewhere in the large company of family members.

Three days passed before Jesus' parents realized the lad was nowhere to be found. Hurrying back, they were amazed to discover that Jesus had remained at the Temple, and was sitting among Hebrew teachers, answering their questions. Luke wrote of this moment: "So when they saw Him, they were amazed; and His mother said to Him, 'Son, why have You done this to us? Look, Your father and I have sought you anxiously.' And He said to them, 'Why is it that you sought Me? Did you not know that *I must be about My Father's business?'* " (Luke 2:48–49, italics added).

So Christ's first recorded words include a divine absolute. This imperative emphasized His *commitment to duty*. And the "Father's business" was the redemption of humanity.

In this we discover a second principle for the intercessor: *To be like Jesus, I must do God's business.*

Christ prefaced His call to His first disciples with the words "Follow Me and I will make you fishers of men" (Mark 1:17). God's business might be discussed in countless ways, but the bottom line cannot be avoided: Jesus came, lived, and died for the redemption of humanity. Saving souls is the Father's "business," and intercessors committed to doing the Father's business will keep world evangelization high on their list of personal prayer priorities.

Three: A Commitment to Mission

Thus, our next divine imperative from the great Intercessor deals with mission. Of His preaching tour in certain desert cities near Capernaum, Luke said: "Now when it was day, He departed and went into a deserted place. And the crowd sought Him and came to Him and tried to keep Him from leaving them; but He said to them, '*I must preach the kingdom of God to the other cities also,* because for this purpose I have been sent' " (Luke 4:42–43, italics added).

Here, Christ emphasizes His commitment to the ultimate mission of His life, that of establishing the Kingdom of God—everywhere.

Jesus had concluded His ministry at Capernaum and was about to move into a desert place when a crowd of people hurried after Him. They had witnessed the impact of His ministry with the many accompanying miracles occurring wherever Jesus went, and they wanted more. Which is like some in the Church today who want to hoard the blessings of God. Consider those growing congregations that build huge edifices to accommodate their remarkable growth, with the intention that later, vast sums of money will be available for missions. But somehow when that day arrives new local projects arise, further delaying the release of such resources.

But note Christ's reaction to those who would hoard the blessings: "I must preach the kingdom of God to other cities also."

Here we discover our third priority principle for intercessors:

To be like Jesus, I must go somewhere with the Gospel.

It is a principle that emphasizes *a commitment to mission.* All believers are commissioned to become involved in the Great Commission. The Church is called to go into all the world. Everybody, everywhere, must be evangelized. And in order for the Church to go *everywhere,* every believer must go *somewhere.*

For many this can best be done on our knees! That's why we refer to this principle as a commitment to *mission,* singular, rather than a commitment to *missions,* plural. All of us have a specific mission in life. No matter what we do in reference to the Great Commission, we should never look at it in a purely general sense. Missionaries do not go into all the world; they go individually into specific parts of the world. Thus, they impact all the world collectively. But only as we accept our individual mission as an intercessor will we make a contribution to evangelizing "all the world."

Four: A Commitment to Endurance

As Jesus continued His ministry throughout the cities and villages near Jerusalem, the hour approached when He was to sacrifice His life on the cross. As He ministered in one of the villages, a group of Pharisees came to Him with the stern warning, "Get out and depart from here, for Herod wants to kill You" (Luke 13:31).

Jesus responded promptly, "Go, tell that fox, 'Behold, I cast out demons and perform cures today and tomorrow, and the third day I shall be perfected.' Nevertheless, *I must journey today, tomorrow, and the day following;* for it cannot be that a prophet should perish outside of Jerusalem" (Luke 13:32–33, italics added).

When Jesus spoke of His being perfected on the third day, He was referring to His encounter on the cross that would take place just three days later. These were to be trying days, days that would include Gethsemane's warfare, His betrayal, and Calvary itself. Any ordinary person, knowing such warfare awaited, would probably have retreated to a place of solitude to rest before the battle. But Jesus had a job to do and He was going to preach His way to the cross. When told to go into hiding for fear of Herod, Jesus responded with the imperative, "I must journey today, tomorrow, and the day following." It was His way of saying, "I must keep persevering until My appointed time arrives!"

At the heart of intercession is a spirit of perseverance—a quality Christ demonstrated in these final ministry encounters. In so doing He was providing us a basis for our fourth priority:

To be like Jesus, I must refuse to quit. Christ was showing us that ultimate victory required *a commitment to endurance.*

Jesus knew He was going to die in three days. And yet He recognized there was yet work for Him to do. Indeed, even on the cross His earthly ministry continued as He reached out in love to the dying thief.

Note especially the word *perfected* in Luke 13:32. From the Greek word *teleioo,* "perfected" means to complete or finish a task or assignment, or to bring something to a desired end. Christ was going to work faithfully in His final days on earth, ever persevering, until He could "perfect" or "complete" His ultimate work on the cross at Jerusalem.

Such is the picture of the true intercessor. Perseverance is the key to their commitment. It is, by definition, the willingness to continue a course of action in spite of the difficulty or opposition. True intercessors, like Jesus, function from a commitment to endurance.

Five: A Commitment to Relationship

One day Christ's ministry brought Him to the thriving city of Jericho where large crowds had gathered to see Him. Word of His miracles drew throngs hoping for a glimpse of this Galilean preacher. One, a Jericho tax collector of short stature, inched his way through the crowd. Zaccheus was fascinated by what he had heard of this miracle-worker and finally decided to climb a tree to see for himself.

Luke explains: "And when Jesus came to the place, He looked up and saw him, and said to him, 'Zaccheus, make haste and come down, for today *I must stay at your house*' " (Luke 19:5, italics added).

Jesus wanted a personal encounter with Zaccheus. He saw the worth of this lone soul, and was willing to invest whatever time was necessary to introduce him to the Gospel of the Kingdom.

Christ cares about people, a quality vital to the lifestyle of an intercessor. To Zaccheus He expressed the concern in His words, "Today I must stay at your house." It seems to be just a passing remark but it contains another priority for would-be intercessors:

To be like Jesus, I must care about people!

Jesus had made *a commitment to relationship.* He wanted to be close to people. Note that He didn't say, "Zaccheus, I'm holding a series of meetings at the Temple this weekend; I hope to see you there." Jesus went straight to the house of Zaccheus. He met him where he lived.

Most people do not find Christ at an evangelistic meeting but because someone relates to them right where they live. And even those who do find Christ while attending a church gathering usually are drawn there by a friend who has taken the time to relate to that person's need.

How much more effective modern-day evangelism would be if we returned to the New Testament pattern of house-to-house ministry. In Christ's encounter with Zaccheus, the tax collector's entire household was affected by Christ's visit. The intercessor who touches just one person with the Gospel where he or she lives may be touching an entire generation with Christ's message of eternal life.

Six: A Commitment to Sacrifice

Intercession and sacrifice are closely related. As stressed earlier, death to self is essential to intercession. Jesus used the divine absolute in referring to His sacrifice on the cross: "And as Moses lifted up the serpent in the wilderness, *even so must the Son of Man be lifted up,* that whoever believes in Him should not perish but have eternal life" (John 3:14–15, italics added). Employing the third person, Christ refers to Himself as "the Son of Man" who "must be lifted up."

Often this verse has been used by preachers to challenge believers to "lift Jesus" so the world might be drawn to Him. Actually Christ made this statement in reference to His being lifted on the cross. He was making a parallel to Moses' day when a plague swept God's people and Moses was instructed to lift up a serpent on a tree. This was a clear look at the future power of the cross to destroy the serpent's plans.

Here Christ provides us yet another priority principle: *To be like Jesus, I must pick up my cross daily.* The cross represents *a commitment to sacrifice,* a quality vital to intercession.

Paul also pictured this principle when he wrote, "But what things were gain to me, these I have counted loss for Christ. But indeed I also count all things loss for the excellence of the knowledge of Christ Jesus my Lord, for whom I have suffered the loss of all things, and count them as rubbish, that I may gain Christ" (Philippians 3:7–8).

The cross is the perfect picture of intercession. Here we see Jesus, who will soon take up His position as eternal Intercessor at God's right hand, hanging between heaven and earth as a go-between or mediator. As intercessors who bear our own crosses of sacrifice, we too stand between hurting humanity and a loving Father, carrying their concerns to God in prayer.

Seven: A Commitment to Opportunity

Try this simple exercise in opportunity awareness. Pause a moment, close your eyes, and quietly quote John 3:16 from memory.

It probably took you no longer than ten seconds to say, "For God so loved the world that He gave His only begotten Son, that whoever believes in Him should not perish but have everlasting life." Sadly, in that same time, an estimated fifteen people will die. That's 5,400 people in the next hour, or more than 130,000 by this time tomorrow—and half of them have no knowledge that Christ died for their sins.

What a tremendous need for intercession these figures present! We should never miss an opportunity to minister. Jesus certainly is our model here. He recognized the value of the moment. He never missed an opportunity to minister. When He encountered a man who had been blind since birth, His disciples were interested in the cause of this infirmity. "Rabbi," they asked, "who sinned, this man, or his parents, that he was born blind?" (John 9:2).

But Christ saw the situation from a different viewpoint. "Neither this man nor his parents sinned," Jesus responded, "but that the works of God should be revealed in him." He then added, *"I must work the works of Him who sent Me while it is day;* the night is coming when no one can work" (John 9:3–4, italics added).

Here we find another priority principle of Christ for the intercessor:

To be like Jesus, I must do something today! It expresses *a commitment to opportunity* and a sense of divine urgency.

An experience involving a dedicated Every Home for Christ field worker in Brazil years ago illustrates. The worker, distributing simple printed Gospel messages, walked up the busy streets of a shopping area, sharing literature and engaging in conversations about Christ whenever possible. One such conversation occurred in a barber shop. The worker was witnessing to a man who was receiving a haircut when the barber himself began to ask questions. In moments the barber came under unusual conviction and asked if he might receive Christ as personal Savior right then. So while a surprised customer sat quietly in the chair watching, the barber received Christ as Savior.

The worker continued visiting shops throughout the district, and as the day drew to a close began to retrace his steps for home. Nearing the same barber shop where earlier he had led the man to Jesus, he noticed a commotion. The entry to the shop was crowded with people. An ambulance waited. The worker couldn't believe his eyes. The very barber he had led to Jesus earlier that day lay dead by his chair. Tears came to the worker's eyes, but they were tears of joy, not of sorrow. He had been at the right place, at the right time, and had seized the opportunity of the moment. And best of all, the barber was in heaven!

Eight: A Commitment to Finishing the Race

Our final intercessory absolute also comes from John's Gospel (see John 10:1–18). Here Jesus portrays Himself as the Good Shepherd who "gives His life for the sheep." He says, "And other sheep I have which are not of this fold; *them also I must bring,* and they will hear My voice; and there will be one flock and one shepherd" (John 10:16, italics added).

Christ was soon to complete His assignment and fulfill His purpose in coming to earth. The cross was only days away. The urgency with which He walked and worked, loved and lived, was now about to culminate in a glorious burst of eternal completion. He would pursue His purpose to the cross—and beyond. His intercession at the Father's right hand, along with our prayer labors on earth in unity with Him, would be a part of His "must bring" plan to touch every tongue and tribe, people and nation (Revelation 5:9).

He would finish what He came to do. And from Christ's longest recorded prayer, in John 17, we find a clarification of this commitment to completion: "I have glorified You on the earth. I have finished the work which You have given Me to do" (John 17:4).

When Jesus said there were other sheep not of this fold that He must bring He was providing us a basis for our final priority principle of Christ:

To be like Jesus, I must finish my assigned task. It is *a commitment to consummation,* consummation being the completion or fulfillment of a plan or goal. What Jesus prayed before the cross, "I have finished the work," was amplified in a word of consummation on the cross: "It is finished!"

Here is the spirit of the intercessor. We will become partners with Christ, our eternal Intercessor, in carrying out the completion of His "other sheep" commitment. We will give, we will go, we will weep, we will work until "every kindred, every tribe, on this terrestrial ball, to Him all majesty ascribe, and crown Him Lord of all!"

four
Ordered Warfare
Establishing Battle Strategies for Intercession

Have you ever felt that Satan has singled you out for special treatment? As if maybe he's breaking in a new demon and needs just the perfect bumbling specimen to practice on and you get the nod! Any follower of Jesus in close touch with God's Word recognizes the reality of unseen satanic forces. They are well-ordered and seek particularly to wreak havoc with our goals of intercession. Surely if Satan has a strategy it would be well for us, as believers, guided by God's Word and Spirit, to cultivate our own strategy.

Order: A Key Tool of the Intercessor

Scripture is very clear about the spiritual importance of setting our prayer lives in order. David, in describing his desire for daily prayer, said, "My voice You shall hear in the morning, O Lord; in the morning I will direct it to You, and I will look up" (Psalm 5:3).

Charles Spurgeon wrote of this passage,

> If we merely read our English version of this text, and want an explanation of these two sentences, we find it in the figure of an archer—"I will direct my prayer unto Thee." In other words, "I will put my prayer upon my bow, I will direct it toward heaven, and then when I have shot up my arrow, I will look up to see where it has gone."
>
> But the Hebrew expression here has a much fuller meaning than "I will direct my prayer." It is the word that is used for the laying in order of the wood and the pieces of the sacrifice upon the altar, and it is used also for the putting of the showbread upon the table. It means just this: "I will arrange my prayer before Thee." I will lay it out upon the altar in the morning just as the priest laid out the morning sacrifices. I will marshal up my prayers. I will put them in order. I will call upon all powers available, and I will pray with all my might, acceptably.

The Hebrew word employed here for "direct" is *arak*. From this word we derive our English word *arrange*. *Arak* is a word frequently used in the Old Testament and wherever used it speaks of establishing order at some level or degree.

As Spurgeon suggested, a most frequent use of *arak* in Scripture concerns the order that priests brought to their daily sacrifices. Note God's instructions to Moses in establishing Tabernacle worship: "You shall put in it the ark of the Testimony, and partition off the ark with the veil. You shall bring in the table and *arrange* the things that are to be *set in order* on it . . ." (Exodus 40:3–4, italics added). The

word used for both *arrange* and *set in order* in this passage
is the Hebrew *arak*.

Scripture is saying that wisdom sets things in order
before coming to the Lord with our intercessions. Proverbs
says that wisdom has "furnished her table" (Proverbs 9:2).
In this case *furnished* means "arranged." The Scripture is
saying that wisdom sets things in order just as a table is
properly arranged for a meal. Isaiah also used *arak* when
he said, *"Prepare* the table; set a watchman in the
tower . . ."* (Isaiah 21:5, italics added). Here *arak* is used to
picture an ordered preparation prior to establishing a
watchman in the tower.

Notice the spiritual warfare implications in these passages, especially interesting to us as intercessors. Jeremiah, too, employs *arak* in a warfare context when he
prophesies, *"Order* the buckler and shield, and draw near
to battle!"* (Jeremiah 46:3, italics added). Here *arak* is
translated "order."

Especially interesting regarding the use of *arak* in a
battle setting is the confrontation between Israel and
rebellious Benjamin as recorded in Judges 20. Concerning
Israel's battle plan against Benjamin, it says they "put
themselves in battle array to fight against them . . ."
(Judges 20:20). To establish a "battle array" (*arak*) means to
develop an ordered strategy prior to entering the conflict.

Note the significance this holds for the intercessor. We
must be prepared prior to our going into each battle.
When Job said, "See now, I have *prepared* my case, I know
that I shall be vindicated," he used the word *arak* (Job
13:18). A primary definition of *arak* in the Hebrew lexicon
is to set in order a cause in a court of justice.

In sum, *we need to work out a plan of attack prior to engaging
the enemy in warfare prayer.* There is nothing unscriptural

about praying with order. To say, "I pray as the Holy Spirit leads me," sounds good but can become a copout for neglecting ordered, intelligent intercession. Indeed, veteran intercessors demonstrate a deep dependence on the Holy Spirit for power and direction in prayer but likewise recognize that the Holy Spirit will give both order and insight to help us pray effectively. Much on the pages to follow is designed to assist intercessors in developing just such biblical order to their praying.

Strategies for Victorious Warfare

Strategy is a plan of action. Three foundational Bible passages guide us to basic strategies for victorious warfare.

First, *as intercessors we should consider Peter's call to vigilance*. Peter wrote, "Be sober; be vigilant; because your adversary the devil walks about like a roaring lion, seeking whom he may devour. Resist him, steadfast in the faith . . ." (1 Peter 5:8–9). *Sober* used here means we are to be self-controlled in light of our enemy's continuing designs to destroy us through myriad temptations. *Vigilant* means watchful, a reminder that we are to be alert. The use of the word *resist* is especially important. It is from the same Greek word translated "stand" in Paul's challenge to the Ephesians: "Stand therefore, having girded your waist with truth . . ." (Ephesians 6:14). *To resist* simply means to take a stand. And it's not merely a passive, defensive stand. It's an offensive stance that seeks to send the devil running.

Second, *as intercessors we should consider James' call to resistance*. He declared, "Therefore submit to God. Resist the devil and he will flee from you. Draw near to God and He will draw near to you" (James 4:7–8). Here the word *resist* is from the Greek *anthistemi,* meaning to stand against or oppose. It is from the same root used in Paul's warfare chapter (Ephesians 6) in which he tells us to "stand against [*histemi*] the wiles of the devil."

Noteworthy in James' challenge is his linking of submission and prayer to victorious warfare. You might call it James' "warfare sandwich." The apostle's "resist the devil and he will flee from you" is sandwiched between *submission* ("submit to God") and *prayer* ("draw near to God"). This latter challenge is especially vital because it speaks of our intimacy with the Father. And the closer we come to God, the further the enemy has to flee. Satan most fears the presence of God.

Third, *as intercessors we should consider Paul's call to preparation.* The apostle began his admonition with the twofold call "Be strong in the Lord" and "Put on the whole armor of God" (Ephesians 6:10–11).

Paul then systematically outlined the nature of our spiritual conflict, the structures of invisible beings in the heavenlies, and the importance of being properly equipped for the coming warfare. It is here that he used the analogy of armor to show us precisely what is needed by believers in order to prepare adequately for Satan's attacks.

Of particular interest concerning our arsenal of spiritual equipment is that each aspect of the armor is an analogy—except one. For example, we cannot actually see our breastplate of righteousness or our shield of faith. They are types or analogies of realities that can be understood only in spiritual terms. Nor can we actually take into our hands a literal helmet of salvation. But this is not the case with the last aspect of our armor, the sword of the Spirit, which is the Word of God. We can take God's Word literally into our hands and employ it as a spiritual weapon. This is what Jesus did in His wilderness warfare when His repeated response to Satan's suggestions was, "It is written" (see Matthew 4:4, 7, 10).

Our "it is written" is the Word of God employed in prayer. The Word, in fact, is actually the only offensive weapon listed in Paul's arsenal of spiritual weaponry. All other aspects of the armor are defensive.

Following Paul's challenge to put on the whole armor of God, including taking up the sword, the apostle declared, "Praying always with all prayer and supplication in the Spirit, being watchful to this end with all perseverance and supplication for all the saints—and for me . . ." (Ephesians 6:18–19).

Here we discover an important truth: *Prayer isn't so much another weapon on our list of weaponry as it is the actual battle itself.* It is the arena of conflict in which we engage our enemy. In concluding his challenge to Ephesian believers regarding spiritual warfare Paul provided us a unique sixfold strategy.

A Call for "Continual" Intercession

Paul introduced his prayer warfare strategy with the challenge to "pray always." In another letter the apostle said, "Pray without ceasing" (1 Thessalonians 5:17).

Paul was not suggesting, of course, that anyone pray twenty-four hours a day, but rather that we continue in a state of readiness to pray as needs arise. The expression *without ceasing* is from the Greek *adialeiptos,* a word commonly used in ancient Greece to describe someone with a hacking cough. The person certainly couldn't plan his coughs throughout the day but coughed whenever necessary. The need occasioned the response.

So it is with seasoned intercessors. Like the cough that comes when the urge arises, prayer is offered for each need encountered.

To pray without ceasing can be used both as a personal and corporate intercessory discipline. Few accounts are more thrilling than the record of the great hundred-year prayer meeting established by Moravian believers in 1727. Persecuted Christians from Bohemia and Moravia sought refuge in 1722 at the estates of Count Nikolaus von Zinzendorf, a devout nobleman living in Saxony (modern Germany). Zinzendorf had named the community Herrn-hut, meaning "the watch of the Lord."

Sadly, during the first five years of Herrnhut's existence the community scarcely resembled its name. By the begin-ning of 1727, Herrnhut, now numbering about three hun-dred, was racked by dissension. Any hope of revival was out of the question. In desperation, Count Zinzendorf and others covenanted to seek God for one of the most basic focuses of all intercessory prayers, spiritual awakening.

And then on May 12 it happened. An unusual visitation of God swept through Herrnhut. In days, all dissension disappeared, every unbeliever was converted. Of those days, the Count would later say, "The whole place repre-sented a truly visible habitation of God among men."

The entire community was seized by a spirit of interces-sion. By August 27 twenty-four men and twenty-four women had covenanted to spend one hour each day in intercessory prayer, thus sustaining continuous prayer. Before long, many others made similar commitments. On and on the intercessions went, month after month, year after year, decade after decade. Quoted in *Decision* mag-azine, historian A. J. Lewis relates: "For over one hundred years, the members of the Moravian church all shared in the 'hourly intercession.' At home and abroad, on land and sea, this prayer watch ascended unceasingly to the Lord."

The Moravians' spirit of intercession took on tangible form as they started sending missionaries abroad. Within the first two years of beginning their intercession for the nations, twenty-two Moravian workers had died. Future Moravian missionaries would refer to that season as "the Great Dying."

But still they persisted, and still they prayed. Within sixty-five years the Moravians dispatched three hundred missionaries throughout the world. Some of their victories, indeed, altered history. Just eleven years after the beginning of the continuing prayer watch, for instance, a young man troubled by deep spiritual doubts and apprehensions wandered into a Moravian prayer meeting in London. Years later he would say of that night that his heart was "'strangely warmed" as he came to a personal knowledge of Jesus Christ. The man's name was John Wesley, and the rest is history.

A Call for "Complete" Intercession

Paul's prayer strategy follows with the phrase *with all prayer*, an expression *The Amplified Bible* translates *with all manner of prayer and entreaty*. We are to include all manner of biblical prayer as a part of our spiritual warfare.

There are many types of biblical prayer that can be categorized. In the mid-'70s the Lord asked me to "watch" with Him one hour each day (see Matthew 26:41), and because He showed me twelve categories of prayer, I realized that devoting just five minutes to each theme would equal one hour.

Naturally this was only a guide, and when sharing this concept with others I've always been cautious not to convey a sense of legalism.

The complete list, which subsequently became the book *The Hour that Changes the World* (Baker Book House, 1978), includes the following:

1. *Praise*—a time of *exaltation!* The psalmist said, "Because Your lovingkindness is better than life, my lips shall praise You" (Psalm 63:3). To praise God is to acknowledge Him for who He is. It is to exalt God with our words. Praise ought to be the entry point for all prayer.

2. *Waiting*—a time of *adoration.* Although closely related to praise, waiting is a time of silently adoring God for who He is. The psalmist said, "I wait for the Lord . . . my soul waits for the Lord more than those who watch for the morning" (Psalm 130:5–6). Whereas praise means to acknowledge God in words for His greatness, waiting is more a time of just loving Him in silence.

3. *Confession*—a time of *examination.* This is a time devoted to personal evaluation of our spiritual status as believers. The psalmist said simply, "I acknowledge my sin . . . I will confess" (Psalm 32:5). Paul told Corinthian believers, "Therefore having these promises, beloved, let us cleanse ourselves from all filthiness of the flesh and spirit, perfecting holiness in the fear of God"(2 Corinthians 7:1). Confession is our part in the cleansing process. Christ's part is the cross.

4. *Scripture praying*—a time of *appropriation.* Balanced prayer needs time in God's Word. We should read the Word and pray the Word. This might be labeled "promise praying." It is to take the Word of God, which generates faith, and appropriate that faith through our praying.

Through Jeremiah God said of His Word, "Is not My word like a fire? And like a hammer that breaks the rock in pieces?" (Jeremiah 23:29).

5. *Watching*—a time of *observation*. Here time is devoted to cultivate a silent alertness regarding issues needing prayer. Soon we will be interceding for others and petitioning God for ourselves. Watching helps us prepare for these focuses. Paul taught believers to "continue in prayer, and *watch in the same* with thanksgiving" (Colossians 4:2, KJV, italics added).

6. *Intercession*—a time of *intervention*. No devotional hour could ever be complete without at least some time being set aside to minister in prayer on behalf of others. Intercession is essentially compassionate warfare. It is to intervene in someone else's battle. Note Paul's appeal for compassionate warriors: "Strive together with me in your prayers to God for me; that I may be delivered from them that do not believe in Judaea" (Romans 15:30–31, KJV).

7. *Petition*—a time of *expectation*. Petition focuses on our personal needs. It might be described as the verbalizing of our desires to the Lord. More than fifty passages in the Psalms, for example, include expressions like *Cleanse me, Help me,* or *Strengthen me.* Jesus emphasized petition when He said to His disciples, "What things soever ye desire when ye pray, believe that ye receive them, and ye shall have them" (Mark 11:24, KJV).

8. *Thanksgiving*—a time of *appreciation*. Another important aspect of ordered prayer is thanksgiving. The psalmist said, "Enter His gates with thanksgiving" (Psalm 100:4). Paul, too, showed this to be an important aspect of prayer when he wrote, "Devote yourselves to prayer, being watchful and *thankful*" (Colossians 4:2, NIV, italics added).

9. *Singing*—a time of *edification*. Singing need not be tied exclusively to corporate worship. This aspect of worship not only exalts the Lord but edifies the believer. The psalmist sang, "My lips shall greatly rejoice when I sing to You" (Psalm 71:23). When Paul told believers to be filled with the Spirit, which brings edification, he added, "Speaking to one another in psalms and hymns and spiritual songs, singing and making melody in your heart to the Lord" (Ephesians 5:19). In several places in Scripture we see the ministry of music linked with effective spiritual warfare (2 Chronicles 20:20–22; Acts 16:25–26).

10. *Meditation*—a time of *investigation*. Another significant aspect of prayer is meditation. This involves a spiritual investigation of God's nature and character as revealed in His Word as well as in creation. The psalmist said, "I meditate on all Your works" (Psalm 143:5). Specifically, meditation is to probe the nature of God, His ways, His acts, and His deeds with careful intensity. When focused on God's Word it is to investigate a passage carefully, searching out all hidden truth. The psalmist also said, "In His law doth [the godly man] meditate day and night" (Psalm 1:2, kjv).

11. *Listening*—a time of *revelation*. Listening, too, is a type of prayer necessary for a balanced warfare strategy. It is a quiet receptivity that allows God to reveal to us what might be called revelation insight concerning the activities of each particular day. Paul spoke of this receptivity when he prayed for the Ephesian believers "that God . . . may give to you the spirit of wisdom and revelation" (Ephesians 1:17).

Listening, of course, is but one of the several silent

aspects of prayer on our list. Because these silent prayer focuses seem similar, it is important to understand how they differ. Waiting, which is our first quiet aspect of prayer, is to *love* God. Meditation, also a silent prayer focus, is to *study* God. Listening, on the other hand, is to *hear* God. Thus, all three of these focuses, though quiet in nature, have uniquely differing functions.

12. *Praise*—a time of *jubilation*. We return to the place where we began in prayer—praise! We do this because Christ taught us to begin and end our prayer with praise (see Matthew 6:9, 13, KJV). But whereas we began with a time of *exaltation* in praise, we now conclude with a time of *jubilation* in praise. Seasoned intercessors recognize the significance of cultivating a spirit of rejoicing in prayer. Take time to rejoice! Be jubilant! And remember, true worshipers never run out of focuses for praise. The psalmist said, ". . . I will hope continually and will praise You yet more and more" (Psalm 71:14).

As you develop the above steps, or any other patterns for intercession, cautiously avoid dead, ritualistic praying, which is prayer without the Holy Spirit. Spiritual alertness will help you stay sensitive to the Holy Spirit's promptings.

If you use the above twelve steps, keep in mind that several may overlap. For example, you might sing the Word in prayer, which combines Scripture praying and singing. If you first meditate on the passage to be sung, you're adding meditation to that prayer. And if all this is focused on a nation, such as the singing of a song from Scripture over a nation, claiming that God's glory will touch that land, you've added yet another aspect of prayer, intercession.

Indeed, it is truly possible to use a plan and yet keep it fresh.

A Call for "Energized" Intercession

Paul's warfare strategy continues with his admonition to pray with "supplication in the Spirit." Supplication represents an intense form of intercession. *Deesis,* the Greek word for *supplication* (Ephesians 6:18), refers to continual, strong, incessant pleading.

James pictured this level of prayer when he wrote, "The effectual, fervent prayer of a righteous man availeth much" (James 5:16, KJV). The Greek word translated "effectual" in this passage is *energeo,* from which we derive our word *energy.* James was speaking of prayer energized by the Holy Spirit. Perhaps this is why Paul referred not merely to supplication in his Ephesian strategy but to supplication "in the Spirit." It is fervent intercession "supernaturalized" by the Holy Spirit.

We also see this level of intensity linked to our Lord. The author of Hebrews tells us Christ "offered up prayers and supplications with strong crying and tears" (Hebrews 5:7, KJV). Here we note that the word *supplications* is plural. Christ's prayer intensity was not a one-time emotional display in Gethsemane the night before Calvary. His intercessions were filled constantly with the energy and intensity of the Holy Spirit.

A Call for "Sensitive" Intercession

After Paul challenged believers to pray with "supplication in the Spirit," he added the injunction, "being watchful." As stated earlier, watching in intercession is to develop a sensitive alertness to the Holy Spirit's promptings. The intercessor must know what to pray for. Paul told Roman believers, "For we do not know what we should pray for as we ought, but the Spirit Himself makes intercession for us . . ." (Romans 8:26).

Earlier in the verse Paul said, "Likewise the Spirit also helps in our weaknesses." The Greek word translated *helps* is one of the longest New Testament Greek words— *sunantilambanomai.* The word means "joint help." It describes the strength and assistance afforded by any two persons who are working together. Another definition is "the mutual bearing of the same load by two people." This suggests that the Holy Spirit does not do all the work for us in prayer but works with us! It is a joint effort. As we depend on God's Spirit in prayer, He will show us how and what to claim in prayer.

A Call for Persistent Intercession

Next, Paul instructed warriors to pray with "all perseverance." This two-word expression, from the Greek *proskartero*, means "to adhere firmly to" or "to be in close pursuit of an object sought." It also means "to be always intent on the goal before you."

The combination of these meanings would suggest a spirit of intercession that never forgets its true purpose. We're not praying just to appear more spiritual. Nor are we praying to gain blessings. Our goal is much greater. *We are reaching out in prayer with the supreme purpose of seeing Christ's Kingdom ultimately established throughout the earth.* And to that end, we must persist. All God's promises must be taken at face value. Like Daniel who persisted for many days because he was intent on his goal (Daniel 10:2, 12–13), intercessors must develop a quality of faithful persistence.

Noah is a perfect example. From the Genesis account of the flood (see Genesis 5–6) we discover that one hundred years passed from the time God warned Noah of a flood until the actual first rains that caused it. Imagine the potential self-doubt coupled with the almost certain ridicule and criticism! Still, Noah persisted in building something no one had ever seen before, an ark, to prepare for something no one had ever experienced before, a flood. And it took a full century. Little wonder Scripture reads, "Noah was a pleasure to the Lord" (Genesis 6:8, TLB).

A Call for "Focused" Intercession

Paul's warfare strategy concludes with a twofold appeal for focused prayer. He pleads, "Pray always with all prayer . . . for all saints and for me." Paul was suggesting both a *general* focus ("for all saints") and a *specific* focus ("for me").

A general focus for prayer might include praying for general categories of needs regarding God's work and those who sustain it. To pray for several countries each day in prayer, for example, asking God to strengthen and bless Christian work and workers in those countries, is a general focus. Fuel for this kind of praying can come from various sources, including newspapers, TV newscasts, even church bulletins or regular missionary magazines. Of course, the more detail this information includes, the more one moves toward a more specific focus, which Paul emphasized by his appeal to pray "for me, that utterance may be given to me, that I may open my mouth boldly to make known the mystery of the Gospel . . ." (Ephesians 6:19).

It is significant that when Paul appealed personally for

prayer, he didn't request material blessings, such as finances or health, but the right words and boldness to proclaim the Gospel. Here again we see prayer's primary priority—glorifying Christ throughout the world and thereby "bringing many sons to glory!" (Hebrews 2:10). Indeed, prayer that scarcely mentions missions is prayer missing the very heartbeat of God. "God," after all, "so loved the world that He gave. . . ."

five
Authoritative Intercession:
Keys to "Fasting" Down Strongholds

Fasting. It might be called prayer that isn't fun!

Describing a particularly intense encounter with this aspect of prayer, Martin Luther said, "My flesh was wont to grumble dreadfully."

Of course, consistency in prayer at any level is difficult. That's because, as a child once wrote, "Satan trembles when he sees the weakest saint on his knees."

But of all the levels of intercession, this one seems to terrify our enemy the most. It saturates our petitions with an authority that comes in no other way.

To combine fasting with intercession is to add special power to our prayer. It is authoritative praying that allows us to "fast" down enemy strongholds.

Authority is defined as power to influence or persuade

from knowledge or experience. It is also the legal or rightful power to command or act in specific situations.

How does fasting relate to intercession? Intercession is the denial of self in prayer so that our praying is focused on others; and fasting is a physical form of humility and self-denial for which Scripture indicates special power. Fasting in conjunction with intercessory prayer is authoritative praying at its highest level.

Fasting, of course, is the practice of deliberately and voluntarily abstaining from usual nourishment, which, when performed in the context of prayer, brings supernatural power to our praying. Fasting is to do without, or to practice self-denial. Its meaning can be expanded to include temporary abstinence from anything in order to give more concentrated attention to spiritual matters. Scripture reveals five distinctive aspects of this difficult-to-understand category of "authoritative praying."

Brokenness in Intercession

First, *fasting is a personal, voluntary humbling of the heart before God that increases spiritual brokenness.*

The psalmist said, "When I wept and humbled myself with fasting, I was jeered at and humiliated" (Psalm 69:10, AMPLIFIED). The New English Bible reads, "I have broken my spirit with fasting."

Humility is at the heart of fasting. Humility is a quality that manifests itself in how one acts in relation to God and others. It is to lower one's estimate of self by elevating one's estimate of others.

And because fasting carries this quality of humility into the tangible, physical realm, it brings about a brokenness before God that can come in no other way. Such brokenness not only honors God but makes the intercessor's heart more pliable to hear from Him. He is thus more useful in carrying out God's Kingdom plans.

Control in Intercession

Second, *fasting is a commitment to self-control that enables a believer to die to self.*

Paul spoke of *temperance* (or self-control) as a fruit of the Spirit (Galatians 5:23). Temperance is the quality of moderation in one's appetite and passions. It is to take control over one's flesh by not allowing anything to grow to the point of excess. In this case it is to put to death that which is impure or excessive.

Note how fasting amplifies this action. The psalmist said, "But as for me, when [my enemies] were sick, my clothing was sackcloth; I afflicted myself with fasting, and I prayed with head bowed on my breast . . ." (Psalm 35:13, AMPLIFIED).

Afflicted is a strong word in the text that might equally be translated *torture.* Surely anyone who has fasted any length of time can readily identify with the use of this expression to describe fasting.

But the *New English Bible* suggests an even stronger translation: "I mortified myself with fasting," which could be paraphrased, "I put myself to death." Fasting truly helps us die to self, and death to self is the key to spiritual vitality and productivity.

In an age in which so many believers (prominent spiritual leaders included) are succumbing to the works of the flesh, surely a fresh call to fasting and prayer is in order.

Could it be that fasting is the key to overcoming Satan's

increased attacks on the moral well-being of even our spiritual leaders?

Paul certainly understood his need to keep his body in subjection. He said to the Corinthians, "I beat my body and make it my slave so that after I have preached to others, I myself will not be disqualified for the prize" (1 Corinthians 9:27, NIV.) Paul wasn't speaking of engaging in some form of penance for his failures but of maintaining self-control when confronting fleshly desires. And certainly this chief apostle knew that fasting and prayer was high on the list of maintaining that authority.

Receptivity in Intercession

Third, *fasting is a worship activity that increases spiritual receptivity by creating a climate for the Holy Spirit to speak.*

Fasting often brings a heightened sensitivity to those making personal or corporate decisions.

The author of Acts described such a circumstance regarding the sending forth of laborers: "As they ministered to the Lord, and fasted, *the Holy Ghost said*, 'Separate me Barnabas and Saul for the work whereunto I have called them.' And when they had fasted and prayed, and laid their hands on them, they sent them away" (Acts 13:2–3, KJV, italics added).

Here we see the combination of a spirit of worship with a spirit of fasting. Another translation reads, "While they were worshiping the Lord and fasting . . ." (NIV).

Not only did the disciples see the worth of fasting as they faced the issues of reaching the lost, but as the result of their fast they were able to receive specific guidance from the Holy Spirit. Indeed, it is possible that had they not fasted, the Holy Spirit might not have spoken.

Ezra, too, recognized the power of fasting in seeking guidance. When the scribe proclaimed a fast prior to leading God's people from their Babylonian captivity (see Ezra 8:21–23), he noted three specific focuses for the fast:

First, Ezra called the people to humble themselves before God and seek of Him a "right way for us." Guidance was clearly the first focus for their fast.

Second, they sought God with fasting regarding the care of their "little ones."

Finally, God's people sought the Lord with fasting for protection of "all their possessions."

In looking at the details of this fast, we immediately note the significance of the first focus. Ezra knew it was possible that enemies would attack them along the way. Already he had told the king they needed no military escort. But suddenly the reality of the situation faced Ezra squarely. Ordinary prayer wasn't enough. A time to fast and pray was essential. Fasting is a key to hearing "the right way"!

Power in Intercession

Fourth, *fasting is concentrated spiritual preparation for Holy Spirit-empowered service that increases the believer's spiritual power.*

Recall the baptism of Jesus as pictured by Luke: "Then Jesus, being filled with the Holy Spirit, returned from the Jordan and was led by the Spirit into the wilderness" (Luke 4:1).

Here we note that Jesus was "led" into this season of fasting by the Holy Spirit. God's Spirit must always be our Guide as we encounter any level of spiritual warfare.

Jesus' fasting lasted forty days, during which time Satan

confronted Him repeatedly. But Christ returned "in the power of the Spirit" to Galilee. Note how this differs from Luke's earlier words that Christ was "filled with the Spirit" before going into the wilderness (see Luke 4:14).

This seems to suggest that whereas Christ was filled with the Spirit before the fast, after the fast, He went forth in the power of God's Spirit, with the Spirit flowing out of Him. Jesus went into the wilderness with internal power, but He emerged with external power.

Something had happened during those forty days of fasting that brought added spiritual power. And significantly, that power was first released during the fast itself to thwart Satan's attempts at leading our Lord into temptation. Thus, Jesus not only defeated Satan with the power of the Word—"It is written"—but with the power of a fast that surely amplified the employment of the Word.

In all this we discover again that Christ is our supreme example of an intercessor. And here we see Him fasting His way to victory. Thus, those who would ask to be like Jesus will sooner or later follow His leading to a life sprinkled with seasons of prayer and fasting.

Ministry in Intercession

Finally, *fasting is a specialized service ministry that increases spiritual usefulness for the totally committed believer.*

One of Scripture's most remarkable women considered fasting her calling. The Bible says, "Now there was one, Anna, a prophetess, the daughter of Phanuel . . . of a great age, and had lived with a husband seven years from her virginity; and this woman was a widow of about eighty-four years, who did not depart from the temple, but served God with fastings and prayers night and day" (Luke 2:36–37).

Interestingly, the Authorized Version's expression "there was *one* Anna" (italics added) has special significance. Of the Bible's 2,989 characters mentioned by name, there indeed is only one Anna. Further, she has a ministry no one else is pictured as possessing. Anna served God by praying and fasting day and night.

Naturally, this is not to say Anna never ate or slept. God never calls anyone to a level of ministry that requires such intensity of effort that ends up destroying the very temple (our bodies) that He has commanded us not to destroy (see 1 Corinthians 3:16–17).

But it is interesting to note that the Scripture refers to Anna's "fastings" and "prayers" in the plural. This suggests that Anna experienced recurring occasions of sustained fasting and prayer. Note also the phrase *night and day*. Anna was sensitive to the Holy Spirit's direction, even if it meant sustained times of prayer at night. Fasting and prayer was Anna's specialized ministry as a committed believer. It is a calling available to any believer who would begin his or her ministry of prayer and fasting with periodic appointments with the Lord, during which self is denied for a portion of a day (or even an entire day or two) as the Lord leads.

Fruitful Fasting

Any who would seek an entry into this exciting ministry of fasting and prayer would do well to follow several simple suggestions:

First, *we should fast sensibly*.

A danger of discussing only those Bible characters or historic Christian leaders who engaged in sustained times of fasting, like seven, twenty-one, and forty days, is that we appear to be picturing prolonged fasts as the norm. The fact is, Scripture often refers to fasts of twenty-four hours or less.

Note, for example, Israel's battle with the rebellious tribe of Benjamin. When Israel saw the circumstances and feared the worst, they "went up and came to the house of God and wept. They sat there before the Lord and fasted that day until evening" (Judges 20:26). David fasted in a similar fashion (2 Samuel 3:35), as did Cornelius, the centurion, who fasted until "the ninth hour," which was mid-afternoon (see Acts 10:30). In all of these cases the fast was twenty-four hours or less.

John Wesley, when establishing the Methodist Church, considered fasting so important that he required all candidates for ordination to fast until 3:00 P.M. on Wednesdays and Fridays. Wesley realized that fasting and prayer for even a portion of a day made a difference.

So one need not begin a personal ministry of fasting and prayer by setting unrealistic goals. Begin simply, perhaps with the denial of one or two meals each week. To fast until 3:00 P.M. would mean to deny oneself breakfast and lunch that day. It may not seem like much to those who speak of fasting twenty-one or forty days, but your stomach will let you know within moments that even the missing of a single meal is a denial that brings the body into subjection.

Second, *we should fast secretly.*

When addressing the subject of fasting in His Sermon on the Mount, Jesus said; "Moreover, when you fast, do not be like the hypocrites, with a sad countenance. For they disfigure their faces that they may appear to men to be fasting. Assuredly, I say to you, they have their reward. But you, when you fast, anoint your head and wash your face, so that you do not appear to men to be fasting . . ." (Matthew 6:16–18).

Christ was not suggesting we never tell anyone we intend to fast. Family members need to know why we are not coming to meals, as do friends who might wonder why we have suddenly stopped usual fellowship. Rather, Jesus was chiding people who tried to appear more "spiritual" than they really were by pretending to fast. The text does not say the hypocrites fasted but that they tried to look as if they were fasting. To fast secretly, then, has more to do with humility than with secrecy.

Third, *we should fast sensitively.*

When Israel fasted prior to its battle with Benjamin, we note they "inquired of the Lord" during their fast (see Judges 20:26–27). One of the most important results of fasting is that it increases our sensitivity to guidance. This sensitivity can be cultivated more richly by including significant seasons in God's Word during a fast.

Fourth, *we should fast systematically.*

When Jesus taught His disciples about fasting, He began with the easy-to-overlook phrase "When you fast" (Matthew 6:16). Notice He did not say, "If you fast." Christ was making it clear that fasting was to be part of their ongoing spiritual development. And for this to happen in a meaningful way, we should consider a systematic approach to times of fasting.

To fast systematically is to set aside time on a regular basis for the purpose of drawing near to God with fasting and prayer. It may involve one day a week, or one day a month, or even a portion of a day. The key is that the fast be on a regular basis.

For several years in our ministry, hundreds of intercessors have helped us sustain a continuous fast for spiritual awakening and world evangelization. Each takes one day a week or month to fast and pray for the Church and her mission to reach a lost world. They don't pray that entire day but they do fast and pray sometime during that day.

Because these intercessors help our ministry break through difficult barriers, we call them "Breakthrough Partners." Many churches are responding to this call and are encouraging entire congregations to participate in their own sustained times of fasting. It can easily be accomplished if just a handful of people take a specific day, or portion of a day, on a systematic basis.

Seven people, for example, each fasting a different day a week, would cover the week. Only 31 persons, each taking an assigned calendar day per month, would also make possible a continuous fast. All it takes is coordination and a little spiritual creativity and discipline. Posting a large, plastic-covered handmade calendar, for example, on which names could be added or removed, helps stir up others to enlist.

Fifth, *we should fast sacrificially.*

Of fasting Andrew Murray said, "Fasting helps to express, to deepen, and to confirm the resolution that we are ready to sacrifice anything, to sacrifice even ourselves, to attain what we seek for the kingdom of God."

For the person who normally skips breakfast, to offer to miss the breakfast meal for a time would hardly be a sacrifice. To sacrifice is to deny oneself something for the sake of another. The hunger pains we feel during a fast serve to remind us that self-denial is indeed taking place. No doubt fasting brings power because it costs us something we can feel.

Sixth, *we should fast specifically.*

When God chided His people for the hypocrisy and

emptiness of their spiritual celebrations, including their fasting, He concluded: "Is this not the fast that I have chosen: to loose the bonds of wickedness, to undo the heavy burdens, to let the oppressed go free, and that you break every yoke?" (Isaiah 58:6).

God must choose the focus of our fast. We recall how the disciples fasted specifically before sending Barnabas and Saul on their missionary journey (Acts 13:2–3). It was a focused fast. Ezra, too, had clear direction as he fasted before leading the people from captivity back to Jerusalem (Ezra 8:21–23).

When moving into a fast, ask the Lord to give you clear direction concerning His purposes for the fast.

Finally, *we should fast supernaturally.*

A special characteristic of fasting is that it requires trust and confidence in God. The very nature of fasting requires dependence on God's supernatural power to see us through.

Note again the corporate fast of those involved in the mission of the early Church. The Scripture says that while they worshiped and fasted, "the Holy Spirit came!" (Acts 13:2–3). Their sacrificial fast brought a supernatural visitation of the Holy Spirit, during which specific directions were given.

The Gift of Wednesdays

Have you ever considered giving a loved one the gift of fasting?

Just before Christmas seven years ago, I asked God to show me what I could give our two daughters, Dena and Ginger, for Christmas. "A gift, Lord, that will touch them for the rest of their lives."

What a strange prayer! It was almost as if it had not come from me at all but from God Himself. What could I possibly give two teenagers that would touch them every day of their lives?

Then I heard a distinct question whispered in my heart: *Are you willing to give your daughters a year of Wednesdays?*

I was baffled. Did God want me to cancel my schedule for every Wednesday during the coming year so I could spend more time with the girls? I knew the idea was impractical. On many Wednesdays I would be out of town in ministry. On others the girls would have school activities.

Then I seemed to hear a further clarifying question. *Could you set aside every Wednesday as a time of fasting for your two daughters?*

I went numb. "O Lord, I could never do that!"

Why? came the gentle response.

"For one thing," my heart answered, "I'd forget."

Not if you mark every Wednesday on your calendar as a fast, the Lord suggested. *During the day when you'd normally be having a meal, you could pray.*

"But there's another reason I couldn't fast like that," I added hastily. "I really, sincerely don't want to, Lord!" And I chuckled.

But I knew God had talked to me. *Come,* He was saying. *Let Me teach you a way of prayer you have never known.*

So I said yes to Christ that day seven years ago. As the weeks passed a new habit was formed, one that continues to this day. I am convinced that our daughters have had a spiritual hedge about them as they encountered the personal problems of youth.

And I am convinced that the greatest single help in building that hedge was the Lord's suggestion that I give our children the gift of Wednesdays.

A Company of Givers

Those who fast follow in the footsteps of a glorious company . . . Moses, the Lawgiver; David, the king; Ezra, the teacher; Elijah, the prophet; Daniel, the prime minister; Nehemiah, the statesman.

Fasting believers keep company with Luther, Calvin, Knox, and John Wesley; they walk with Jonathan Edwards, David Brainerd, Charles Finney, and Hudson Taylor.

But most of all, they walk in the steps of Jesus who denied Himself through fasting, and who continues to give of Himself as our chief Intercessor at God's right hand.

six
Praying for the Lost
Monday: Six Interrogatives of Intercession

In evaluating a balanced strategy of intercession, seven distinct categories emerge. Although appropriate any day, they may conveniently be assigned to the seven days of the week for a practical plan of intercession.

The first category, our Monday focus, is lost souls. World evangelization and the Great Commission represent a biblical theme not limited to the New Testament. When the people of Israel brought the Ark of God into the midst of the Tabernacle, for example, David offered a beautiful psalm that included the admonition, "Proclaim the good news of His salvation from day to day. Declare His glory among the nations, His wonders among all peoples" (1 Chronicles 16:23–24).

Before His ascension into heaven, Christ commissioned

His disciples to "go therefore and make disciples of all nations, baptizing them in the name of the Father, and of the Son, and of the Holy Spirit, teaching them to observe all things that I have commanded you . . ." (Matthew 28:19–20).

Sadly, as we meditate today on these passages, nearly half the population of the world waits for word of Christ's love. Needed is an army of committed intercessors who will intercede for the lost so they may have access to the Gospel of Jesus Christ.

The Example of Jesus

But to approach this subject intelligently, we first need to address a question: Are we really given authority to pray for the lost? Consider this paraphrase of Christ's High Priestly Prayer:

> "I am not praying for these alone, but also for the future believers who will come to me because of the testimony of these. My prayer for all of them is that they will be of one heart and mind, just as you and I are, Father—that just as you are in me and I am in you, so they will be in us, and the world will believe you sent me."
>
> (John 17:20, TLB)

Isaiah painted this picture of the coming Messiah: "And He was numbered with the transgressors, and He bore the sin of many, and made intercession for the transgressors" (Isaiah 53:12). *The Living Bible* reads, "He was counted as a sinner, and he bore the sins of many, and he pled with God for sinners."

To plead for sinners is to pray for the lost.

Note also Paul's admonition: "Therefore I exhort first of all that supplications, prayers, intercessions, and giving of thanks be made for all men . . ." (1 Timothy 2:1–2). The call for intercession on behalf of "all men" clearly includes the lost. The passage goes on to declare that God "desires all men to be saved and to come to the knowledge of the truth" (v. 4).

So we have clear biblical authority to pray for the lost. How might we proceed?

Shortly after returning from my first trip to mainland China, I began praying daily for Chinese people to hear about Jesus. But I faced the problem of how to pray for people I did not know who lived in cities whose names I couldn't even pronounce.

Praying for wisdom (James 1:5), I was promptly reminded of a passage in Romans revealing how unregenerate man by nature keeps some of the Law even if he's never heard it (Romans 2:14). Of God's judgment Paul said: "He will punish sin wherever it is found. He will punish the heathen when they sin, even though they never had God's written laws, for down in their hearts they know right from wrong. God's laws are written within them; their own conscience accuses them, or sometimes excuses them" (Romans 2:12–14, TLB).

So there were points of contact with these unknown people, places where the Law was already inscribed on their hearts. Thinking on these words, I asked the Lord to give me a plan of prayer that would make contact with that place in their hearts.

Suddenly, the six interrogatives I learned as a youth in English class came to mind: *who, what, when, why, where,* and *how.* I knew God had given me these interrogatives to help me pray.

Whom Can I Trust?

First, I could intercede for lost souls by praying that they be confronted with questions regarding trust. I might ask that God would plant in the hearts of lost people a skepticism about the lies they hear, whether philosophical, social, or political.

This is especially appropriate when praying for people in oppressed nations of the world like Communist or Muslim nations. We can pray that political leaders will do things that cause distrust throughout their areas. Once people begin feeling distrust, they will wonder whom they really can trust. Soon they will discover it is not possible to trust anybody other than someone who is absolutely perfect. Eventually this search will direct their thoughts toward God.

What Is My Reason for Being?

I might also intercede for unevangelized people by praying that they begin to ask, "What is my purpose for living?" Ask God to plant in their hearts an urgency concerning this question. This will cause a reevaluation of their reason for being and lead them to consider a purpose not found at a human level. This will likewise direct the person's attention heavenward.

When Will I Really Be Free?

When interceding for people where there is relatively little freedom, we can pray that God will use this lack to draw people to Himself.

When praying for lost souls in Muslim nations we might change this question slightly to ask, "Am I really free?"

Muslims do have a deep faith but need to recognize they are not really free from sin. Pray they will feel an emptiness that can be satisfied only by receiving Christ into their lives.

When interceding for the lost in free nations, we might pray that the person will ask, "When will I be free of this emptiness in my heart?"

Why Do People Reject God?

The fourth intercessory question concerns the reality of God. This prayer interrogative relates especially to those who live in atheistic countries. Ask God to cause lost souls to question why their leaders so vehemently reject the existence of God. Asked often enough, this question leads people on a deep heart-quest. They will not only wonder if there is a God; soon they will actively seek after Him.

Some two years after praying these interrogatives, I read about a Soviet fighter pilot who defected to Japan in his MIG jet. I was amazed to read that almost all six of the interrogatives on our list were questions the pilot had been asking for months leading up to his defection. The final question concerned God's existence. For weeks he had been asking, "Why, if our government leaders are so convinced there is no God, must they fight so intensely against the idea of His existence?" His reasoning led him to the conclusion there must be a God, and a short time later he defected.

How Can I Cope with My Problems?

This interrogative of intercession applies to all lost souls for whom we pray. We may ask God to plant a sense of hopelessness in their hearts. Every person faces some problem beyond his abilities. Our prayers of intercession would cause these people to realize their need for deliverance and thus prepare their hearts for the day the Gospel will be given to them.

We realize, of course, that praying these prayer interrogatives does not force salvation upon an individual, but rather prepares his or her heart for the Gospel. Intercession, indeed, is vital for the preparation of all hearts that ultimately receive salvation. Rare is the believer who does not know the person or persons who prayed for his or her salvation.

Where Will I Go When I Die?

Finally, we might ask God to cause unbelievers to ask, "Where will I go when I die?"

The reality of death is understood in every culture. Everyone wonders about death at some point in life. Indeed, in poorer regions of the world the reality of death is ever close. We should pray that God will turn these questions into a quest for an eternal answer, that He will plant a longing to resolve the issue. Imagine the reaction of one for whom we are praying if one evening he asks, "Where will I go when I die?" and the next day he receives a Gospel booklet on eternal life!

Do Something!

The more we study intercession, the more aware we become of the vast scope of this spiritual activity. Any of the patterns presented on these pages could absorb an entire intercessory hour. Veteran intercessors know that the more we are touched with a burden, the more time it takes. It becomes easy to understand how Anna grew into a full-time intercessor (see Luke 2:36). Anna was able to fast and pray day and night because she was touched with the great concerns of those around her.

Applied to our praying, we must be touched with the ultimate burden of God's heart, the total evangelization of the world and the resulting completion of the Bride of Christ. When this happens His Kingdom will come! (See Matthew 24:14; Revelation 11:15.)

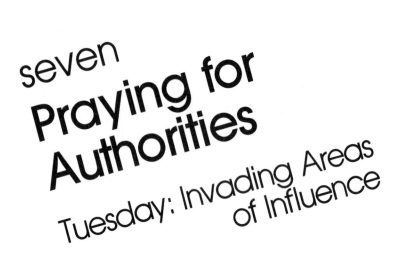

seven
Praying for
Authorities
Tuesday: Invading Areas
of Influence

Paul admonished Timothy to pray for "all who are in authority, that we may lead a quiet and peaceable life in all godliness and reverence" (1 Timothy 2:2).

Interceding for our leaders, Paul suggests, will result in our being able to follow the commands of Christ so that people everywhere will know His love. This conclusion is borne out in Paul's summation that God "desires all men to be saved" (1 Timothy 2:4).

A Primary Focus

It is clear from Scripture that the spiritual health of a nation is related to the spiritual health of its leaders. In Proverbs we read, "With sensible leaders there is stability" (Proverbs 28:2, TLB.)

When taking the reins of leadership from David, Solomon declared, "You know how my father David could not build a house for the name of the Lord his God because of the wars which were fought against him on every side, until the Lord put his foes under the soles of his feet. But now the Lord my God has given me rest on every side; there is neither adversary nor evil occurrence" (1 Kings 5:2–4).

It is almost impossible to fulfill God's *ultimate* plan for a nation if it is constantly embroiled in conflict. This is why we pray for peace. Generally speaking, a climate of peace is the best climate for evangelization. And because the spread of the Gospel is most hindered in repressed nations because of restrictive laws enacted by their leaders, we must make these leaders a primary focus for our prayers.

Praying the "Micah Plan"

In Micah 6:8 we find the basis for what I call the Micah Plan to help us pray for world leaders. Here Micah describes the lifestyle and conduct of a leader: "He has shown you, O man, what is good; and what does the Lord require of you but to do justly, to love mercy, and to walk humbly with your God?" (Micah 6:8). From these words emerge three simple focuses to help us pray for leaders.

First, we must pray that a particular leader will "do justly." This is to pray that he or she will govern *truthfully, with a spirit of sincerity.*

When the Bible speaks of doing what is just, it is speaking of one's carrying out his or her functions on a foundation of that which is truthful and right. The word *just* means ethical, equitable, and fair. Thus, we can pray that a leader will be drawn toward that which measures up to these important qualities.

Second, we may pray that a leader will "love mercy." This means he or she will govern *compassionately*, with *a spirit of generosity*. "To love mercy" is to conduct oneself humanely. Pray that God will cause leaders to be flooded with a spirit of unselfishness mixed with much loving-kindness toward their subjects.

Third, we may pray that the leader will "walk humbly with God." This means he or she will govern *modestly*, with *a spirit of sensitivity*. These qualities are in direct conflict with the roots of original sin, a spirit of pride. As Scripture declares, "Pride goes before destruction, and a haughty spirit before a fall" (Proverbs 16:18). It was a haughty spirit that caused Lucifer to fall. And it is a haughty spirit that causes leaders to fall. Our prayers for leaders, then, should include warfare against all forms of pride and arrogance that might diminish that leader's effectiveness.

Concentrated Warfare

Because the Micah Plan features several *generalized* prayer focuses, it is important that we share a variety of specialized prayer focuses for intercessors who wish to conduct more concentrated warfare for those in authority.

First, we can pray that *unjust leaders* will make mistakes that help advance the Gospel of Jesus Christ. The psalmist prayed concerning unjust accusers: "Make them fail in everything they do. Clothe them with disgrace" (Psalm 109:29, TLB). The King James relates, "Let them cover themselves with their own confusion."

Missionaries have often testified how doors have been

opened for evangelistic activities simply because of mistakes made by leaders. In one Communist nation, for example, the government sought ways to lessen the political impact of the Catholic Church. At that very time Every Home for Christ, over which I serve as president, was seeking permission to take Bibles house-to-house throughout their nation. Thinking that allowing a Protestant group such freedom would undermine the Catholics, the government agreed. The fact was, the Catholics were delighted that tens of thousands of people in their land would receive Bibles.

Second, we can pray that *tyrannical leaders* will fall from power by receiving unsound advice.

When David cried out concerning those who were persecuting him, he declared, "Pronounce them guilty, O God! Let them fall by their own counsels" (Psalm 5:10). *The Living Bible* reads: "O God, hold them responsible. Catch them in their own traps; let them fall beneath the weight of their own transgressions, for they rebel against you."

Is it God's will for evil leaders to fall from power? What we read in God's Word is His will. If we are convinced, according to His Word, that a particular promise applies to a situation, we ought to claim that promise with total authority in that situation. Thus, if we see a tyrannical leader insanely directing a nation away from God, killing multitudes of its people in the process, we have every right to pray like David, "Catch them in their own traps!" We should pray that the snares these tyrannical leaders set for others will turn against them.

Third, we can pray that all *godly leaders* will discover spiritual wisdom to govern their nations.

Not all leaders are godless. Some are genuinely searching for truth, as in this paraphrase from Proverbs: "Where
there is moral rot within a nation, its government topples
easily; but with honest, sensible leaders there is stability"
(Proverbs 28:2, TLB).

Many world leaders may have had the seed of truth
planted in their hearts. Usually this will manifest itself in
small ways, alerting sensitive intercessors to pray. When
such evidence arises, we should pray that these seeds will
grow up to produce spiritual wisdom to help these leaders
govern righteously.

Fourth, we can pray that *all leaders* will receive a
personal message of God's love.

After Isaiah spoke of "beautiful feet" bringing good
news (Isaiah 52:7), he said of the Messiah, "So shall He
sprinkle many nations. Kings shall shut their mouths at
Him; for what had not been told them they shall see, and
what they had not heard they shall consider" (Isaiah 52:
15).

We know it is God's will that all people come to a
knowledge of salvation. We have the assurance then, that
we are praying in God's will when we ask that all leaders
will receive knowledge of God's love. For years ministries
like Every Home for Christ (formerly World Literature
Crusade) have sought various means to communicate the
Gospel with leaders at the highest level. Hundreds of
specific acknowledgments of either Gospel messages, Bibles, or other Gospel communications have been received
from such leaders. Seeds have been planted and the
possibility of future fruit exists if we pray.

Fifth, we can pray that *leaders in troubled nations* will
grow weary of the continuing bloodshed in their lands.

We recall again David's inability to build the Temple because of wars about him (see I Kings 5:3–4). We should ask God to put on the hearts of leaders in these troubled lands the recognition that they need help from a higher Source.

Sixth, we can pray that *corrupt leaders* will recognize their evil ways and turn to God.

When Manasseh, king of Judah, was bound and carried into Babylon, his affliction caused him to humble himself and turn to the Lord (2 Chronicles 33:11–13). We might pray for corrupt leaders to encounter circumstances that would draw them to the Lord.

Finally, we can pray that *all leaders* will realize that God alone gave them their positions of authority.

Picturing God's sovereignty, Daniel said, "Blessed be the name of God forever and ever, for wisdom and might are His. And He changes the times and the seasons; He removes kings and raises up kings; He gives wisdom to the wise and knowledge to those who have understanding" (Daniel 2:20–21). Because God alone places leaders in their positions, and God alone has the power to remove them, we need to pray that these leaders will recognize this fact and know they must answer to God.

Interceding for Areas of Influence

Not all prominent leaders of a land, of course, come under the category of government. There are at least eight distinct areas of influence in modern society for which we can find authority figures needing prayer. Ask the Holy Spirit to show you which specific area you might include on a regular basis in your times of intercession.

They include:

1. *The political arena.* This area of influence includes elected or appointed officials involved in every aspect of government. Under this category would come presidents, prime ministers, dictators, and all political advisors who might help shape decisions regarding a nation. Also included would be such groups as those involved in Islamic courts (which make key laws), the Soviet Politboro, and such groups as a Communist Party Central Committee. Under any of these categories, naturally, the list of specific political functions could be rather long. As intercessors we should ask the Holy Spirit to lead us to His choice of specific focuses in any of these categories.

2. *The judicial arena.* This focus includes those responsible for interpreting and enforcing the laws that govern a land. We should pray for our judges, courts, and law enforcement agencies. In some countries, military leaders also might come under this category because they also have responsibility for maintaining law and order.

3. *The spiritual arena.* The Bible tells us to pray for *all* who are in authority. This means we need to remember such authority figures as pastors, priests, rabbis, mullahs, ayatollahs, and other religious leaders. If they are not believers, we should contend for their salvation. If they do know Jesus, we should pray for their growth and integrity. Consider the tremendous influence certain evangelical leaders have developed in recent years through the use of television and radio. Little wonder Satan has sought to bring disgrace to this vital area!

4. *The educational arena.* This area of influence includes teachers at every level, from grade school to graduate

school. It is at the earliest level of teaching that children begin to form concepts that will dictate how they will think and live in later years. Parents who believe in the power of prayer ought to maintain a regular prayer list of the teachers instructing their children.

5. *The cultural arena.* This vast area of influence includes such categories as the entertainment industry, the arts, and sports. Entertainers attract the attention of millions of people throughout the world, and ought to be the focus of intelligent, systematic prayer by committed intercessors.

6. *The commercial arena.* Business and the media, which we combine in the commercial category, desperately need concerted intercession. The commercial arena includes influential people in advertising and the media, including television, radio, and newspapers, as well as all who may be involved in leadership positions related to the industrial complex of a nation. Key corporate executives and television news personalities ought to be included on the prayer lists of those intercessors called to concentrate on this arena.

7. *The civic arena.* Although closely related to the first area, there are so many influential leaders serving civic governments that a special category is reserved just for them. True, these leaders occupy political positions, but because they are not in what we generally consider the primary political roles, such as high-level government positions, we often neglect to pray for them. They are essential, however, to the health and morality of the community and are worthy of continuing prayer.

8. *The social arena.* This final category touches all leaders of influence over any kind of group that might not be included under the previous seven. It includes prominent

leaders over social groups, clubs, even fraternities and sororities. Even a family unit, with the head of that household, would come under this classification. Note again Paul's words: "All who are in authority."

As we take up the mantle of intercession "for all in authority," we are hastening the day that Christ's Kingdom will fully come and peace will indeed reign on earth.

eight

Praying for Nations

Wednesday: Confronting Enemy Strongholds

There are some 235 geographical entities we call nations,* and of these an estimated 97 are all but closed to conventional resident missionary activity. More than three billion people live in these 97 so-called "closed" nations. If they are to have access to the Gospel, a miracle of intercession must take place.

The intercession must be both fervent and all-encompassing if we are to see this miracle released in our generation. "God be merciful to us and bless us," says the psalmist, "and cause His face to shine upon us, that Your

---

* By *nation* I refer to all geographic entities that might be considered distinct countries. Some may be protectorates of larger nations, as Guam is to the United States, but because of their distance or isolation from the protectorate, we call these *nations* or *countries*.

way may be known on earth, Your salvation among all nations" (Psalm 67:1–2). Note the three-word phrase *among all nations.* Our intercession must encompass all the world and result in action on our part.

Consider the paraphrase of verse 2: "Send us around the world with the news of your saving power and your eternal plan for all mankind" (TLB). The psalmist isn't just saying, "Send workers, O God," but, "Send *us,* O God!"

The Redemption Factor

John describes a vision of the throne in which a glorious redemption song is sung. As the Lamb (Christ) takes into His hands a great scroll, four living creatures and twenty-four elders fall before Him in worship. Each has a golden bowl filled with incense and the prayers of the saints (Revelation 5:8). John then describes the redemption factor in God's eternal plan with the song,

"You are worthy to take the scroll, and to open its seals; for You were slain and have redeemed us to God by Your blood out of every tribe and tongue and people and nation, and have made us kings and priests to our God; and we shall reign on earth."

(Revelation 5:9–10)

Because the Bible tells us redeemed humanity will come from every tribe, tongue, people, and nation, we know that we are interceding in God's will when praying for all four of these categories systematically in our prayers.

Interceding for "Every Tribe"

From the Greek word *phulee* comes our first focus. *Phulee* is most often translated "tribe," such as the tribe of

Reuben or the tribe of Judah. Because a tribe is not a complete nation, we may conclude that it refers to a smaller group within a nation, such as a cultural group. *Culture* means the totality of socially transmitted behavior or patterns, arts, beliefs, and institutions. Such ethnic groups within a nation have clearly defined patterns of behavior or beliefs that differ from the general population of that nation. If we are to intercede for these people to be reached with the Gospel, we will need methods quite unlike those used to reach others.

The job is enormous. There are an estimated 17,000 such groups scattered around the globe without a resident missionary or functioning church or even an evangelical witness.

How might we translate this opportunity into meaningful intercession?

We must pray for frontier evangelism.

Thankfully, various ministries have responded to the need to evangelize the "hidden people" of the earth. The majority of these ethnic groups can be identified, yet no one has taken the time to go to them with the Gospel. Such pioneer ministries as Every Home for Christ and the U.S. Center for World Missions have sought to mobilize Christians to focus prayers on these groups.

Interceding for "Every Tongue"

From the Greek word *glossa* comes our next prayer category. "Tongue" refers to languages and dialects. During the 1980s Wycliffe Bible Translators passed the 1,000 mark in the number of languages now possessing at least some portion of the Scriptures. There are, however, more than 6,000 known languages and dialects still needing the Gospel, which means much work has to be done. Yet the

Bible says converts will come out of every "tribe *and tongue.*"

To translate this promise into effective intercession, *we must pray for translation evangelism.* Such groups as Wycliffe Bible Translators and Lutheran Bible Translators are working faithfully in this field. P. J. Johnstone's significant manual for intercessors, *Operation World* (Send the Light Publications, P.O. Box 28, Waynesboro, GA 30830), provides names of many other ministries involved in translation evangelism, and is a day-by-day guide to praying for the world.

Interceding for "Every People"

From the Greek word *laos* comes our third focus regarding the nations. Employed 143 times in the New Testament text, *laos* simply means "people." It is a reference to human beings and individuals of a particular race. From childhood we recall the chorus:

> *Jesus loves the little children,*
> *All the children of the world.*
> *Red and yellow, black and white,*
> *They are precious in His sight.*
> *Jesus loves the little children of the world.*

There are three major classifications of races in the world: Caucasoid (white), Negroid (black), and Mongoloid (yellow and red). Veteran missionaries know that to reach a nation they must mobilize the people of that nation, the nationals, to do the task of evangelism. The missionaries simply get the nationals started in the right direction.

Translated into a focus for intercession, *we must pray for national evangelism.* We should claim sound Bible training that equips national believers to reach their own people with the Gospel. We also should pray that conventional missionaries will learn to release authority to those who were raised in that culture.

Interceding for "Every Nation"

The word *nation* in our text is from the Greek word *ethnos.* It appears 164 times in the New Testament and is commonly translated *Gentiles.* The term refers generally to all nations of the world other than Israel.

Nations are usually defined by boundaries. Someday we may understand more fully the spiritual significance of the various geographic borders. It has been suggested that they picture in the visible realm the controlling spiritual forces operating from the unseen realm. God does speak of establishing boundaries in Scripture (Psalm 16:6).

How can we intercede for the nations living within these boundaries? *We must pray for systematic evangelism.* The key word here is *systematic.* We need to pray for all aspects of evangelism that seek systematically to impact a nation, including door-to-door literature evangelism, all plans of personal evangelism, and regularly scheduled radio and TV programs.

To help develop intercession with a systematic emphasis, I have developed a World Prayer Map that divides countries into 31 groups, a different one for each day of the month. The heads of state are listed for these nations, and a list of major world evangelism ministries that serve in all the categories mentioned in this chapter. (For a sample map write to me at P.O. Box 7139, Canoga Park, California 91304–7139.)

Confronting Strongholds

Missionaries who visit the "dark places" of the earth (Psalm 74:20) recognize that certain regions are unusual strongholds of Satan. Satan is at work in every nation, yet it seems he has selected some regions to control more blatantly. We see this especially in Communist and Muslim lands.

When praying for a nation, we should try to determine which satanic strongholds exist there, then exercise our God-given spiritual authority to confront these bastions. The day will come, I believe, when God will reveal specific details about these strongholds to sensitive intercessors. These may include pictures of the controlling forces in the unseen realm that influence Satan's activities in that land.

For now, we do know of several general categories of strongholds deserving special attention.

1. *Government strongholds.* Intercessors should pay special attention to the political characteristics of a nation. Laws decreed by evil governments often hinder the spread of the Gospel. Restrictions imposed by Communist governments especially fit this category. In Albania, for example, the Communist government has added to its constitution an article declaring atheism to be Albania's official state religion. Any other religion is considered a threat to the state—and illegal. Executions have occurred as the result of these restrictions.

One recent report from Albania related how a tourist had left a Bible in the Albanian language at a hotel, hoping it would fall into the right hands. Days later when he was leaving the country, an official handed him the same Bible with the words, "You left this at the beginning of your trip. I am returning it to you, but don't ever do this again."

How do we pray about government strongholds in such difficult political climates? Jesus told us to speak directly to the mountains (Mark 11:23). So *we must pray against the spiritual mountain of satanically inspired laws.* These mountains must be dealt with in the power and authority of Jesus' name.

2. *Cultural strongholds.* Every nation possesses behavioral characteristics. Collectively we refer to these as the culture of a people, and in some cases such characteristics restrict the spread of the Gospel. A spirit of nationalism provides an example. People of a nation may say, "Our way of life is superior to yours." This spirit makes it difficult for someone of another culture to bring the Gospel to those so bound.

The behavioral characteristic of xenophobia, manifested by certain Oriental cultures such as the Japanese or Chinese, provides another example. Xenophobia, a fear of outsiders, causes people to reject those who come from another culture bringing the Gospel.

How do we deal with these cultural strongholds in our prayers? *We must pray against satanically inspired attitudes.* We should ask the Holy Spirit to show us what satanic attitudes exist in a particular nation, and then systematically command these strongholds to be removed.

3. *Religious strongholds.* This focus touches the spiritual characteristics of a land. The Islamic religion is a prime example. It is a religious stronghold seriously hindering the spread of the Gospel in many parts of the world. In addition, there are Buddhism, Hinduism, Taoism, Confucianism, Jainism, Sikhism, Zoroastrianism. Sadly, whereas Christianity is said to have grown 47% in the last 50 years,

Buddhism is said to have grown by 63% and Hinduism by 117% during the same period.

In some countries of the world today it is virtually impossible to engage in open evangelism because of the religious restrictions.

How do we pray against such religious strongholds? *We must pray against satanically inspired beliefs* that enslave entire nations or major people groups of a nation. We must become "new sharp threshing instruments" of the kind God promised to raise up in Isaiah's day: "Behold, I will make thee a new sharp threshing instrument having teeth: thou shalt thresh the mountains, and beat them small, and shall make the hills as chaff" (Isaiah 41:15, KJV).

4. *Material strongholds.* A final focus regarding strongholds in nations concerns the materialistic characteristics of a land.

Some nations appear to be free and have experienced prosperity. Yet there is often lukewarmness in the churches of those nations. Soon apathy toward spiritual things moves a people toward humanism, which puts the emphasis on human development and rejects spiritual values. As with other strongholds, this materialistic spirit can greatly hinder the spread of the Gospel, especially in societies considered free. Mission leaders in Europe, for example, report that evangelism is more difficult in materialistic Western Europe than socialistic Eastern Europe. Materialism is so strong, and its corresponding apathy so great, that many refuse even to listen to the Gospel.

How do we contend with so powerful a stronghold in prayer? *We must pray against satanically inspired ideals.* Direct authority needs to be taken in prayer against Satan's ideals. Social, political, or religious movements that move people toward a materialistic or humanistic view of life should become serious matters for intercessory prayer.

These "mountains," like the others discussed, must be dealt with directly. Intercessors are not just quiet pray-ers. They are mountain movers.

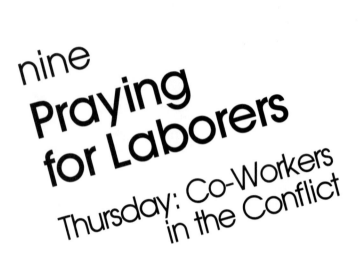

nine
Praying for Laborers
Thursday: Co-Workers in the Conflict

The idea flashed through my mind as I prepared for a trip to Communist Eastern Europe. I needed to take along with me instructors' notes for our School of Prayer, so that leaders there could translate and distribute these materials. But I had heard stories of how Westerners going to this particular region were regularly searched and often had all printed materials confiscated.

I remembered Paul's appeal to Roman believers when he pleaded, "Strive together with me in your prayers to God for me, that I may be delivered from these . . . who do not believe . . ." (Romans 15:30). I needed intercessors not only "striving with me" in a general sense while on this mission, but specifically as I crossed borders into these difficult nations.

114

So I contacted a handful of our most committed inter-cessors scattered across the country and told them the exact time periods involved. I was careful to ask those responding favorably to cover me in prayer for at least one hour before a crossing time and an hour after to allow for the possibility of an early or late arrival. Because of the difference in time between Europe and the United States, many participants would have to get up in the middle of the night.

Yet many responded and soon I had a page full of intercessors' names who had promised to pray with me. Because I wanted to be able to "agree with them in prayer," I carried the list with me on my trip.

Little did I realize how important these intercessors would become. Several weeks prior to my departure, a young Christian courier from Western Europe, working with a group sponsoring my visit, had the assignment of going to the country to set up my schedule. He carried with him a single sheet of paper, carefully hidden, on which were typed all the details of my visit. It included the date of my arrival, the fact that I would be coming from Warsaw, Poland, and my plans to train leaders about prayer mobilization.

Later I learned that the young brother was detained at the border for some four hours and that the authorities had found and confiscated all the details of my visit. Fortunately for me, my full legal name, as it appears on my passport, was not on the sheet. Rather, they had referred to me only with the abbreviation DK (from Dick). Also the sheet did not show the exact details of my flight—only that I was to arrive from Warsaw on the date in question.

Preparing to depart from Warsaw, I had no idea author-

ities would be looking for DK, an American, coming from
Warsaw that day. Naturally, had I been the only American
arriving, they would have known I was that person and
that the DK had been a code. Up to that point, in fact, I *had*
been a lone American struggling to find anyone with
enough English to point me to the correct departure gate.

Suddenly I heard someone speaking in my language
with no foreign accent. Then I heard another, and still
another. I turned to speak to a middle-aged lady who
seemed to be giving instructions to a group. I had taken a
flight filled with American tourists. The lady was a travel
agent from New Jersey and this was an Eastern European
tour her agency scheduled only once every three years.
Now instead of one American on the flight, there were
thirty!

All the while, I carried that slip of paper listing intercessors who even then had been up in the night praying
for me. As the plane taxied down the runway I reached
into my pocket, held the list, and prayed, "I agree with
these who are praying with me now and claim my total
protection."

Upon my arrival I blended in with thirty American
tourists, chatting with those about me as we moved
through immigration.

Then came the tougher task of clearing customs with my
luggage. Before me were five large customs counters. Each
was staffed with an agent searching every bag with vigor.
Knowing how important it is to get just the right agent, I
stopped for a few seconds to pray quietly. I reached into
my pocket and touched the slip—agreeing again with
those who were praying—and chose an agent.

Now I was waiting for the traveler before me to go

through. Every item in his large suitcase was removed and examined. Then the agent grunted and motioned toward another of the man's bags lying at my feet. Stepping to the side to allow the man room to pick up his bag, I found myself facing the agent. We were less than three feet apart. Without a word, the agent snapped his fingers twice, pointed directly at me, and then pointed toward the exit. I knew he was saying, "You can go," and my spirit leaped toward the door, though my body walked casually as if nothing out of the ordinary was happening.

Later I learned the whole story, when I spoke to several Westerners who also had arrived that week. All had been detained, some for as long as four hours, and many had had Christian literature confiscated by customs agents.

In discussing the role prayer played in these circumstances, some said that they, too, had friends praying back home. But when I asked if they knew for certain that those friends had been praying at the exact time of the confrontation, each responded negatively. Nor did they have a list of the intercessors' names to touch, agreeing in prayer. They could only report that friends had promised to pray while they were away.

I knew God had allowed this experience to prove to me the power of agreement in prayer.

The Sentence of Death

Paul spoke of the significance of those who helped him fight his spiritual battles through prayer. To the Christians at Corinth Paul wrote: "For we do not want you to be ignorant, brethren, of our trouble which came to us in Asia: that we were burdened beyond measure, above strength, so that we despaired even of life. Yes, we had the sentence of death in ourselves, that we should not trust in ourselves but in God . . . you also helping together in prayer for us . . ." (2 Corinthians 1:8–11). *The Living Bible* provides this paraphrase: "We felt we were doomed to die" (v. 9).

Not only are we to pray that the Lord of the harvest will "thrust forth" workers into His harvest (Matthew 9:37–38), but we must cover those who already are laboring in that harvest. Paul saw this need. He often spoke of "making mention" of his fellow workers in prayer (see Romans 1:9). One prayer pattern Paul employed for his co-workers is particularly meaningful. It begins: "For this reason we also, since the day we heard it, do not cease to pray for you . . ." (Colossians 1:9). Paul then lists several objectives he desired of the Lord in prayer. We might term these objectives the tenfold "Colossians claims" for Christian workers.

The first set of five claims relates to *a release of revelation:* God revealing His desired results to the worker. The second set of five claims relates to an *increase of blessings* from the Lord for that worker.

Helpful in employing these claims in prayer is to picture oneself as reaching out with both hands to touch the person for whom you are praying. The five fingers of one hand remind us to pray for the first five qualities, while the five fingers of the other hand remind us to pray for the five additional blessings. These ten claims in two sets of five each are:

Revelation

In our first step of intercession for workers, we should claim *a revelation of God's will* for the worker. This claim concerns *divine direction*. Paul prayed that his fellow work-ers would be "filled with the knowledge of God's will." In touching a worker on our prayer list, we need to ask God to reveal His desire concerning that worker for that very day.

Second, we should claim *a revelation of God's wisdom* for that worker. This claim concerns *divine perception*. Paul prayed that the worker would be "filled with all wisdom." Here we ask God to reveal to a worker how he or she might apply God's plan for that day. Wisdom is simply common sense. Spiritually speaking, it's spiritual common sense. One preacher defined it as knowing where you're going and knowing how to get there. Wisdom is to apply practically what we know theoretically.

In our third aspect of intercession, we should claim *a revelation of God's understanding* for the worker. This claim concerns *divine comprehension*. All too frequently Christian workers view problems as man sees them, overlooking God's perspective. Paul prayed that his fellow workers would be "filled with spiritual understanding." To *understand* means to perceive or comprehend the nature and significance of a thing.

In touching a worker, we need to pray that as the result of his experience in the Lord, he will know what he is to do in situations that develop that day.

Fourth, we should intercede for *a revelation of God's holiness* in the worker. This claim concerns *divine perfection*. Paul prayed that Colossian believers would "walk worthy" before God. This means the worker would walk in an understanding of God's holiness as it flows through him or her. One translation of the verse reads: "That you may live a life worthy of the Lord and may please him in every way" (NIV). Here we claim that God's holiness will manifest itself both in and through the worker for whom we pray on this specific day.

Our fifth aspect of intercession claims *a revelation of God's pleasure* in that worker. This claim concerns *divine gratification*. Paul prayed that his fellow workers would walk worthy of the Lord "unto all pleasing." It is to pray that a worker's every act that day would bring gratification to the Lord. Paul longed to see his spiritual friends become treasures to the Lord through their conduct and testimony. Surely this is a quality greatly to be desired by all Christian workers!

Increase of Blessings

After claiming revelation in these five areas, we should intercede for an increase of God's blessing for the worker in five additional categories. They include:

In our sixth aspect of intercession we claim *an increase of effectiveness* for the worker. The focus here is on *increased productivity*. Paul prayed that his fellow workers would be "fruitful in every good work." He was claiming that their effectiveness would increase at every level. When we pray for Christian workers on our list, we should ask God to give them lasting fruit as a result of that day's activities.

Seventh, we should claim *an increase of devotional growth* for the worker. Here the focus is on *increased spirituality*. Paul requests that his fellow Christians would increase "in the knowledge of God." It is possible to increase in our knowledge of God only with a strong devotional life. We should thus pray for each worker on our list that he or she would grow in a hunger for God and His Word.

Eighth, we should intercede for *an increase of strength* for the worker. This focus concerns *increased durability.* Paul desires that his fellow workers would be "strengthened with all might according to God's glorious power." Every worker needs a daily renewal of both physical and spiritual strength. In touching a laborer through prayer, we should claim for the worker a baptism of "fresh oil" (Psalm 92:10).

Ninth, we should claim *an increase of patience* for the worker. This claim touches *increased tenacity.* Tenacity is the quality of holding tightly to a task or promise no matter the circumstance. Paul's desire for his fellow soldiers is that they would be strengthened "unto all patience and longsuffering." Patience is the ability to wait under pressure. Longsuffering is the ability to put up with difficult situations for extended periods of time. Longsuffering is a special form of what might be termed extended patience. Pray that God will give workers on your list a quiet confidence in Him that manifests itself in an increased measure of patience.

Finally we come to the wonderful claim of *an increase of joy* for the worker. This intercession concerns *increased delight.* When Paul says that his companions will be "strengthened unto all patience and longsuffering," he adds, "with joyfulness." The word *joyfulness* in this passage comes from the same Greek word translated elsewhere as "exceeding great joy" (Matthew 2:10).

Note the word *with* in this passage, which shows that all of the claims on this list are to be saturated *with* joy. Fruitfulness should be mixed with joy. Spirituality should be bathed in joy. Strength flows from joy—"The joy of the Lord is our strength" (Nehemiah 8:10). Joy, indeed, is a special ingredient that makes everything we do in Jesus delightful.

We should transfer that joy from our hearts to those on our prayer lists every time we lift them in prayer. One of ancient Israel's statutes declared, "You shall rejoice before the Lord your God in all to which you put your hands" (Deuteronomy 12:18). May we remember that admonition when we daily reach out our hands in prayer, with rejoicing, to touch laborers on the front lines of spiritual battle.

ten
Praying for the Church
Friday: Contending for Spiritual Awakening

One of this century's most significant awakenings began in Wales in 1904, the result of a call to united prayer. According to historian Dr. J. Edwin Orr, Seth Joshua, a Presbyterian evangelist, visited Newcastle Emlyn College in Wales where a young man named Evan Roberts was preparing for the ministry. Roberts was a 26-year-old Welch miner when he felt the call to preach.

During Seth Joshua's visit to the college, the students were stirred to a deep desire for prayer and asked if they could attend his next series of meetings in a nearby city. The request granted, all classes were canceled and the entire student body attended. It was there the students heard Seth Joshua pray passionately, "O God, bend us." Evan Roberts went forward that evening crying out, "O God, bend me."

When the meetings concluded, Roberts returned to the college with his classmates but found he couldn't concentrate on his studies. Something was happening in his heart. "I keep hearing a voice," Roberts told his principal, "that tells me I must go home to speak to the young people in my home church." Roberts wondered if it was the voice of the devil or the voice of the Spirit. The principal answered, "The devil never gives orders like that. You can have a week off."

Young Roberts returned to Loughor and told his pastor he had come home to preach. The pastor was far from comfortable, however, allowing this inexperienced student to address the entire congregation, so he suggested Evan Roberts testify at the prayer meeting on Monday night. Evan agreed, thankful that at least he would have opportunity to speak to some of the congregation.

Attendance was greater than expected at the meeting. The pastor decided not to call on Evan Roberts until the very end. Just before people were ready to depart, the pastor said, "Our young brother, Evan Roberts, feels he has a message for you, if you care to wait."

Only seventeen people remained. Roberts told those present: "I have a message for you from God. You must confess any known sin to God and put any wrong unto man right. Second, you must put away any doubtful habit. Third, you must obey the Spirit promptly. Finally, you must confess your faith in Christ publicly."

According to eyewitnesses, by 10 P.M. all seventeen had responded. The pastor was so moved he asked Evan Roberts if he would be willing to speak at the missions service the following night. Then he asked him to share at the regular Wednesday night meeting. A fourth service was scheduled the following night, and still another. It was decided to continue a second week when the heavens seemed to open.

Soon the main road on which the church was located was packed solid with hungry seekers coming to the service. Shopkeepers even closed early so they, too, could get a seat in the large but packed church.

A Tidal Wave

So powerful was the revival that newspaper reporters were sent to describe the happenings. Like a tidal wave the awakening spread over Wales. In five months 100,000 people met Christ in the immediate region. Judges had no cases to try. There were no robberies, no burglaries, no rapes, no murders. Civic leaders met to discuss what to do with the police now that crime had disappeared. In one community, the sergeant of the police was asked by a reporter, "What do you do with your time?"

"Before the revival," he replied, "we had two main jobs, to prevent crime and to control crowds attending soccer games. Since the revival there is practically no crime. So we just go with the crowds."

When asked what he meant, the sergeant replied, "You know where the crowds are. They are filling the churches."

"But how does that affect the police?" asked the reporter.

"We have seventeen police in our station," replied the sergeant. "Five do nothing but control crowds on their way to prayer meetings."

"What about the other twelve?"

"Oh, we've organized three quartets with those officers," the sergeant responded. "They sing at the churches.

If any church wants a quartet, they just call the police station."

Over the months drunkenness dropped fifty percent; illegitimate births, forty percent in some places. There was even a slowdown in the mines due to the conversion of so many coal miners. Those miners didn't strike; they merely cleaned up the profanity in their language. Horses pulling the carts in the mines didn't understand their "pure" language and had to be retrained.

The Welsh awakening spread throughout the world giving birth to a surge of missionary activity that continues to have impact on the world today.

What an example of revival! The world will be reached for Jesus only by awakened churches that "thrust forth" laborers. That's why Paul told Thessalonian believers that he prayed for them day and night "exceedingly," that he and his co-workers might see them face-to-face and perfect that which was lacking in their faith (1 Thessalonians 3:10). He added: "The Lord make you increase and abound in love one toward another, and toward all men . . . to the end he may stablish your hearts, unblameable in holiness before God . . ." (1 Thessalonians 3:12–13, KJV). These words of Paul provide a unique fourfold prayer pattern specifically touching on interceding for the Church.

The Restoration Focus

First, we must intercede in prayer for the *completion* of the Church. Paul prayed that God would enable him to help "perfect that which is lacking" in the faith of Thessalonian believers. Paul longed to see the Church restored so she might accomplish her supreme task—evangelizing the lost.

When Paul spoke of perfecting the Church, he used a Greek word, *kartartizo*, that elsewhere in the New Testament pictures fishermen mending their nets. Only as their nets were restored or brought to their original condition could they be used again to catch fish.

The same Greek word is found when Paul tells Epaphros, a Colossian believer, that he has labored fervently for him in prayer that he might "stand perfect and complete in all the will of God" (Colossians 4:12). The word is also used in Hebrews 6:1 where we read: "Let us go on to perfection [completion]." In Revelation we discover the Lord's challenge to the seven churches. Speaking to the church of Ephesus regarding restoration, He said, "I have this against you . . . you have left your first love" (Revelation 2:4).

For the Church to fulfill her mission of evangelizing the lost, we must pray for restoration to take place.

The Unity Focus

Second, we must intercede for the *cooperation* of the Church. Paul prayed for a spirit of unity and compassion, that the Thessalonian church would "abound in love one toward another" (1 Thessalonians 3:12).

The early Church *was* united. It was born out of a group of people who were in "one accord" (Acts 2:1). The theme is repeated in Acts when, following an explosive prayer gathering, "the multitude of them that believed were of one heart and one soul" (Acts 4:32).

Paul addressed this theme when later discussing divisions in the churches. To the Corinthians he wrote: "Now I plead with you, brethren, by the name of our Lord Jesus Christ, that you all speak the same thing, and that there would be no divisions among you, but that you be perfectly joined together in the same mind and in the same judgment" (1 Corinthians 1:10).

The word for *abound* in our text (1 Thessalonians 3:12) comes from the Latin *undare,* meaning to rise in waves. Paul was challenging the Thessalonians to allow their love toward each other to rise in great swells, as the waves of the sea rise in response to the tides. Our response to God's love ought to produce waves of love toward our Christian brothers and sisters. If we cannot love those in the Church, we will never love those beyond the Church.

Praise God for thrilling reports of this very spirit of unity presently spreading throughout the Church today! Schools of Prayer, Concerts of Prayer, and interchurch house-to-house evangelism campaigns are uniting thousands of believers in the supreme task of the Church, world evangelization. Intercessors must guard this priceless gift of unity. It is, after all, an answer to Christ's repeated prayer that His disciples would be one (John 17:11, 21).

The Vision Focus

Third, we must intercede for the *commission* of the Church. When Paul prayed that Thessalonian believers abound in love "to all," he was praying that their love for each other would overflow until it had impact on everyone. "All" is not most, or some, or even many. As a preacher once declared, "All means all and that's all all means!" The mission of the Church is to evangelize all the world. And every believer is commissioned to engage in this task.

Christ referred specifically to this commission when He commanded: "Lift up your eyes, and look at the fields"

(John 4:35). Eyes are instruments of vision. Christ was encouraging His disciples to expand the horizons of their inner vision. Later he declared: "Peace be unto you: as my Father hath sent me, even so send I you" (John 20:21, KJV).

Needed in the Church today is an internationalizing of our intercession. Not that we neglect praying for the local church, but that we recognize its significance globally.

One prayer pattern to keep us on target regarding the full sweep of intercession is the Acts 1:8 pattern in which there are three targets for prayer. The *Jerusalem focus* reminds me to pray for those needs close to home, like family, friends, and needs of the local community. The *Judea and Samaria focus* reminds me to pray for needs of my state (or province) as well as my nation. The *"uttermost part" focus* reminds me to pray for activities related to taking the Gospel to distant regions of the world.

The Growth Focus

Finally, we must intercede for the *conviction* of the Church. This concerns spiritual growth in Christ's Body. Numerical growth, though desirable, is meaningless unless the Church grows spiritually. Purity and integrity are essential.

Paul concluded his prayer of desire for the Thessalonians by praying for their hearts to be "unblamable in holiness before God." On another occasion Paul wrote: "Come out from among them [the world] and be separate, says the Lord. Do not touch what is unclean, and I will receive you" (2 Corinthians 6:17).

To Colossian Christians the apostle added:

As you have therefore received Christ Jesus the Lord, so walk in Him, rooted and built up in Him and established in the faith, as you have been taught, abounding in it with thanksgiving. Beware lest anyone cheat you through philosophy and empty deceit, according to the tradition of men, according to the basic principles of the world, and not according to Christ.

(Colossians 2:6–8)

When Paul spoke of being "established in the faith," he used the Greek word *sterizo,* meaning to make firm. We are to engage in those activities that help us firm up our faith. As intercessors, moreover, we should pray that believers everywhere desire new levels of growth that will make this firming up in the faith possible.

eleven
Praying for the Sick and Afflicted
Saturday: Biblical Factors for Physical Restoration

Dealing in prayer with sickness and suffering can be difficult. Almost all intercessors have been confronted with circumstances in which their prayers seemed fruitless. Yet much is said in Scripture about prayer for those who suffer, and no book on intercession would be complete without addressing this matter.

Two words are used by the apostle James when he deals with this matter—*sick* and *afflicted*. He said: "Is any among you afflicted? . . . Is any sick among you? Let him call for the elders of the church; and let them pray . . ." (James 5:13–14, KJV).

Two Greek expressions are used in this passage. *Kakopatheia*, the Greek word translated "affliction," is a reference to anything that causes distress, generally referring to intense suffering caused by circumstances other than illness. In this sense, social distress becomes a focus. The homeless and hungry are not to be forgotten.

In referring to the sick, James uses a different Greek word, *asthenes*, an expression referring to the weak, feeble, or sick.

Thus, in speaking of interceding for the sick and afflicted, we include those who are bound by physical infirmities, but also those oppressed mentally or physically, socially, or spiritually.

Once again we look to Jesus as our supreme example of intercession. Christ had a burden for the sick and afflicted. When Jesus came into the synagogue following His baptism and temptation, He was handed the book of Isaiah and began to read. His words described His own healing mission: "The Spirit of the Lord is upon Me, because He has anointed Me to preach the gospel to the poor. He has sent Me to heal the brokenhearted, to preach deliverance to the captives and recovery of sight to the blind, to set at liberty those who are oppressed, to preach the acceptable year of the Lord" (Luke 4:18–19).

In commissioning His disciples, Jesus appointed them to be healers. "And as you go," He said, "preach, saying, 'The kingdom of heaven is at hand.' Heal the sick, cleanse the lepers, raise the dead, cast out demons. Freely you have received, freely give" (Matthew 10:7–8).

Intercession for the sick is first recorded in Abraham's confrontation with Abimelech when Abraham dwelt in Gerar (Genesis 20:1). Because Abraham feared that telling the truth about his wife, Sarah, might cost them their lives, he lied to Abimelech, saying Sarah was his sister. Abimelech took Sarah to his quarters, no doubt intending to marry her later. That night, however, God came to Abimelech in a dream and pronounced a curse on him and his household because he had approached a married woman.

Abimelech complained bitterly because of Abraham's deception. In fact, he had not yet touched Sarah and God told him he had acted with integrity. But an intercessor was still needed, if the curse was to be lifted. God then told Abimelech, "Now therefore, restore the man's wife; for he is a prophet. And he will pray for you, and you shall live" (Genesis 20:7).

Abimelech obeyed the voice of God and appealed to Abraham. We read: "So Abraham prayed to God; and God healed Abimelech, his wife, and his maid-servants. Then they bore children . . ." (Genesis 20:17).

From such biblical accounts we are able to piece together insights that help us develop a strategy of intercession for the sick and afflicted. Seven factors guide the way.

The Wisdom Factor

First, to intercede for the sick or afflicted we must seek the mind of God for wisdom. "Wisdom is the principal thing," says Proverbs. "And with your wisdom get understanding" (see Proverbs 4:7).

Wisdom is essential. What is the will of God in a

particular circumstance? Jesus taught us to pray, "Thy kingdom come; Thy will be done . . ." but sometimes it is difficult to determine His perfect will in matters regarding physical healing. Some who are sick, for example, need prayer for discipline regarding the proper care of their bodies rather than for a healing of an infirmity caused by that neglect. God looks for healings that last rather than "band-aid solutions" that may lead to worse conditions. God could heal high blood pressure caused by excessive weight in an instant, but He might choose to grant that healing only through the person's discipline of losing thirty or forty pounds. As intercessors, we need wisdom to know how to pray in such matters.

Consider the example of Peter when he was told of the death of Dorcas (Acts 9:39–41). Before Peter commanded Dorcas to rise from the dead, he prayed. Though speculative, this initial prayer could well have been for the wisdom he needed concerning the will of God in the matter. We do know that when Peter finally exercised his authority, he did not ask God to do anything for Dorcas, but rather commanded her to rise.

Wisdom regarding God's will is essential. Years ago I heard the testimony of a Christian mother whose three-year-old daughter had been hit by a car. The doctor's prognosis was bleak. The child would probably die. If she did happen to survive, the child surely would be a "vegetable" as long as she lived.

Shortly after the doctor issued his report, a friend of the mother heard her shout an angry prayer of insistence. "God," she demanded, "either let my daughter live or I will never serve You again!"

The daughter lived, miraculously, but was never able to

think or function beyond the capacity of an infant. Forty years later the mother was still changing her daughter's diapers. She never had even a day to herself for rest and quiet.

Could it be that in God's wisdom it was best to call her daughter home? Surely our Father knows best in these difficult matters and we must seek His wisdom as we pray.

The Willingness Factor

Second, to intercede for the sick or afflicted we must prayerfully determine the willingness of the person to be restored. Some people who suffer do not genuinely long for healing. A person may enjoy receiving the attention an infirmity brings. Others may secretly reject restoration because such healing might require more responsibility on their part.

The willingness factor in praying for the sick must be established if our intercession is to be effective. Pray that the infirm individual will use his or her healing wisely. Ask God to help that person adjust to the ramifications of being well.

The Weakness Factor

Third, to intercede for the sick or afflicted we must seek cautiously to uncover any spiritual weaknesses that may hinder our prayers from being answered.

According to Scripture, sin hinders the potential for seeing God's best released in His children. Isaiah declared: "Behold, the Lord's hand is not shortened that it cannot save; nor His ear heavy, that it cannot hear. But your iniquities have separated you from your God; and your sins have hidden His face from you, so that He will not hear" (Isaiah 59:1–2).

We must avoid being judgmental, but we also need to ask the Lord to reveal any hindrances that might limit the effectiveness of our prayers. Because James linked the confession of sins with physical healing (James 5:16), we have a biblical basis for encouraging the person for whom we are praying to identify and confess any known sins. Seasoned intercessors know that victory over sin is every bit as significant as victory over sickness. Sometimes dealing with sin is the first step in dealing with sickness. Deliverance from sin can be the key to deliverance from disease.

The Word Factor

Fourth, to intercede for the sick or afflicted we must learn to use the power of God's Word as our supreme weapon of attack.

The psalmist linked physical restoration to the power of God's Word when he said: "They cried out to the Lord in their trouble, and He saved them out of their distresses. He sent His word and healed them, and delivered them from their destructions" (Psalm 107:19–20).

In our School of Prayer seminars we challenge participants to bathe their prayers with Scripture. One way to do this is to listen to Scripture on cassettes while you are praying. Take God's promises and declare them in prayer over specific needs on your list.

One School of Prayer participant accepted this challenge and purchased the entire New Testament on cassettes following the seminar. Several days later, while visiting a friend in the hospital, an idea occurred to her for using this new tool. Her friend had been in a coma for many days. Doctors offered little hope of recovery. Nevertheless, the woman sought permission from the head nurse to play cassettes of the Scriptures to her injured friend.

Permission was granted, and a few minutes before noon she placed a cassette player on the bedstand, started it, and headed for the cafeteria for a quick lunch.

While still standing in the cafeteria line, the woman was paged on the hospital intercom and asked to return to her friend's room. She ran upstairs. Her friend was sitting up and talking with a nurse! A twelve-day coma had ended with just a few minutes of recorded Scriptures. God had sent His Word, using a human messenger who believed His promises, and healed her.

The Worship Factor

Fifth, to intercede for the sick or afflicted we must recognize the importance of saturating our prayers with praise and worship.

A spirit of praise is frequently linked to victorious warfare. When God's people were under threat from Moab and Ammon, King Jehoshaphat cried out to God for His strategy for battle. Following a time of sustained worship, Jehoshaphat declared to the people: "Hear me, O Judah and you inhabitants of Jerusalem: Believe in the Lord your God, and you shall be established; believe His prophets, and you shall prosper" (2 Chronicles 20:20). The king then commissioned the singers to enter the battle first. The results were spectacular! We read: "Now when they began to sing and to praise, the Lord set ambushes against the people of Ammon, Moab, and Mount Seir, who had come against Judah; and they were defeated" (2 Chronicles 20:22).

The psalmist also linked worship with warfare: "Let the saints be joyful in glory; let them sing aloud on their beds. Let the high praises of God be in their mouth, and a two-edged sword in their hand, to execute vengeance on the nations, and punishments on the peoples; to bind their kings with chains, and their nobles with fetters of iron" (Psalm 149:5–8). Victory for Paul and Silas in prison also came as the result of prayer mixed with songs of praise (Acts 16:25–26).

My introduction to the power of praise began with a simple song of worship sung over our younger daughter years ago during a serious bout with the flu. Ginger's temperature was 104° and rising when I went into her room to pray. More than a casual prayer was needed.

Recalling the victory of Judah in 2 Chronicles 20:22, I began to sing a song of praise over Ginger. Instantly the fever broke and sweat actually began to pour down her forehead onto my hands.

Years later I shared this experience on television. A woman in California heard the testimony just days before she was to be operated on for a potentially life-threatening condition. At one point her temperature began to rise sharply. Monitors displayed this and other vital signs. Both nurses and family members could see the peril.

Recalling the televised testimony, the woman asked a nurse if her family could sing a song of victory over her. The nurse consented and the family began to blend their voices in praise.

Suddenly all eyes fastened on the monitors displaying the woman's vital signs. A degree at a time the temperature was dropping. The nurse opened her mouth in awe. She had never witnessed anything like it. As the melody ended the display read 98.6. God had met them in their song.

The Warfare Factor

Sixth, to intercede for the sick and afflicted, we must understand and apply principles of spiritual warfare regarding a person's condition.

Much already has been said about developing a warfare strategy in prayer. This certainly applies when praying for the sick or afflicted. As intercessors functioning from a position of authority seated in the heavenlies (Ephesians 2:4–7), we must directly confront the mountain of infirmity before us in prayer (Mark 11:23). We recall again Peter's adventure in authoritative prayer at the Gate Beautiful (Acts 3:1–6).

Peter did not ask God to grant a miracle. He asked God for nothing. Rather, he commanded the lame man directly to rise and walk. His dealing was directly with the infirmity.

Note how Paul told the Ephesians to "stand" against the wiles (schemes) of the devil (Ephesians 6:10–12). Certainly infirmity is a scheme of our enemy to discourage or defeat us. As intercessors we confront these schemes through spiritual warfare. Our stand is not defensive; it is offensive. The disease is our enemy. The name of Jesus is the cure. We must take the cure into the conflict and apply it through our prayers.

The Witness Factor

Finally, to intercede for the sick or afflicted, we must recognize that God's supreme purpose for granting miracles is to reveal Himself. Healing is a witness to the wonder of His Person.

When Jesus and His disciples passed the man blind since birth, as we have already seen, His disciples questioned, "Rabbi, who sinned, this man or his parents, that he was born blind?" (John 9:2). Our Lord responded, "Neither this man nor his parents sinned, but that the works of God should be revealed in him" (John 9:3).

The man's condition was an opportunity for God to reveal the fullness of His power. Miracles open the understanding of many to the mercy of God. Remember, the lame man's healing at the Gate Beautiful resulted in at least 5,000 conversions (Acts 3:1–8; Acts 4:4).

In the Old Testament we also find that God's purpose in answering prayer was to reveal Himself. When Solomon offered his dedicatory prayer over the Temple, he included a petition regarding foreigners in the land. He prayed: "Moreover, concerning a foreigner, who is not of Your people Israel, but has come from a far country for the sake of Your great name and Your mighty hand and Your outstretched arm, when they come and pray in this temple; then hear from heaven Your dwelling place, and do according to all for which the foreigner calls to You, that all people of the earth may know Your name and fear You . . ." (2 Chronicles 6:32–33).

When Hezekiah received an accusatory letter from King Sennacherib denouncing Hezekiah's faith, the king simply spread the letter before the Lord. He then prayed, "Now therefore, O Lord our God, I pray, save us from his hand, that all the kingdoms of the earth may know that You are the Lord God, You alone" (2 Kings 19:19). Again the focus of God's miraculous intervention was that all kingdoms of the earth would know the Lord.

Knowing God is the greatest miracle resulting from our prayers of intercession. In the early years of our twenty-four-hour prayer ministry, I discovered this important secret in a letter of great personal encouragement.

The letter said:

On January 29 I called your ministry for prayer concerning my sister Mary Jane. She had just been hurt in a terrible car accident. We prayed together and the person I talked to on your prayer line said to call back when the miracle happened.

Well, Mary Jane died on the way to the hospital. But since then many miracles have happened. Mary Jane and her husband had been praying for the Lord to use them in any way He so desired to help the people of their small community seek the Lord. Praise God—at Mary Jane's memorial service about fifty people answered the invitation and came forward to receive Christ. Several cousins have made a commitment, and a long-standing bad relationship between our mother and her sister-in-law seems to be mending. Praise the Lord! Mary's absence hurts, of course, but her five children all belong to the Lord, and they seem to be doing fine. I'm sure that there are more miracles to come. Thank you for your prayers.

Could it be that Mary's homegoing was the real miracle in the battle for her healing? Fifty people met Christ at her memorial service. These friends and loved ones saw the miracle of Mary Jane's life in Christ and in that tragedy realized they, too, needed what she had discovered. What initially appeared as an intercessor's defeat was a fiftyfold victory. Mary Jane wouldn't have wanted it any other way.

twelve
Praying for the Family
Sunday: Prayer Patterns for Healthy Homes

I awakened slowly to the sharp jabbing motions of my wife's hand. I could hear Dee muttering, "Who could that be at this hour?"

It was before 7 A.M. Saturday. Our older daughter Dena, six years of age at the time, had invited her friend Sara from next door to spend the night.

Wiping sleep from my eyes, I opened the front door to discover Sara's nine-year-old sister Julie, the oldest of five children in their family. Julie had been crying. She asked if her sister was up yet, and I told her Sara was asleep in Dena's bedroom. Wiping away tears, Julie insisted that Sara come home right away; it was very important.

I awakened Sara and in a few moments she was on her

way. No explanation was given for the sudden intrusion, and both Dee and I wondered if a tragedy had occurred.

Two hours later, around nine, there was another knock on the door. Sara had returned to retrieve some of her belongings left in her hasty departure. Dena was now awake and I could hear the two six-year-olds conversing.

"Why did you have to leave so early?" Dena quizzed.

"My daddy had to talk to us this morning," Sara responded. "He told us all to sit down so he could tell us a hard thing." Sara's voice cracked and it sounded as if she was holding back tears.

"Daddy told us he was going to be leaving our house this morning," she continued, "because he didn't love Mommy anymore." Attempting to defend her father as best she could, Sara added quickly, "But Dena, don't worry about us. He promised he would never stop loving us. He just doesn't love Mommy anymore."

With that both girls burst into tears. One could almost read Sara's mind: "If Daddy really loved Mommy before, and now he's quit loving her, how can I be sure he'll keep his promise to me?"

Prayer was the only hope for healing that home. Scripture assures us victory if we pray in God's will (1 John 5:14–15) and I knew God desires families to stay together. As sure as I know my name, I knew God wanted their daughters raised by a mom and dad who loved one another. So I began to pray.

By the following Tuesday a strange boldness saturated my prayers. Suddenly I felt as if I was confronting a spirit of lust that Satan had used to deceive that husband into desiring a woman who was not his wife. A strange prayer flowed from my lips. I commanded the man to become sick to his stomach, at that very moment, as he faced the reality of his sin. I recalled praying boldly, "Be nauseated in Jesus' name for what you have done!"

Frankly, I couldn't believe those words had come from my lips. But still I knew the Holy Spirit was guiding my prayer.

The confirmation came the following Saturday when I spoke with the young housewife over our back fence. Her face was aglow. "Dick, I have good news! Bob called yesterday for the first time since he left. Something strange is happening. I can't say there's been a total change, but he did tell me he's been feeling funny."

"What do you mean, feeling funny?"

"Well, last Wednesday Bob decided to go see a psychologist for counseling," she explained. "He said he started feeling guilty on Tuesday afternoon as he thought about our girls not having a daddy. It affected his stomach so much he actually became nauseated and felt like vomiting."

The complete miracle was to require a few more days. By the following week, Bob was back and the children had their daddy home.

The Praying Family

Prayer changes homes! Most believers would agree with that. Yet when it comes to translating this conviction into reality, the Church is sadly deficient.

When I first began to develop a teaching on intercession *for* (as well as *in*) the family, I took a trip to our well-stocked local Christian bookstore. I wanted to check out titles related to praying as a family or praying for families. I discovered a multitude of books related to the family, but, to my dismay, nothing that emphasized prayer in or for the family.

I noticed, for example, a book titled *How to Raise Good Kids*. Surely this would include a chapter on prayer. After all, how can we raise good kids without prayer? Yet nothing was included regarding this important subject. Another title read *How to Really Love Your Child*. Prayer certainly ought to be included here, I thought; but again it was overlooked. There was a book titled *Training Your Child to Handle Money*. This might touch on prayer, I thought, since stewardship and prayer go hand-in-hand. But again, prayer wasn't mentioned. I even found the title *Developing Spiritually Sensitive Children*, convinced it would include a chapter on prayer. Again, prayer was all but overlooked.

Only later would I pick up *The Christian Family* by Larry Christensen, and joyfully discover a chapter titled "The Priesthood of Parents," in which the importance of prayer was discussed.

I could not escape the significance, however, of so many books related to enriching family life in which, for the most part, prayer was either totally ignored or mentioned only in passing. Did not so essential a theme deserve better treatment?

A Rock of Remembrance

We recall Joshua's commitment regarding the spiritual well-being of his household when he stood before God's people declaring: "Choose for yourselves this day whom you will serve, whether the gods which your fathers served that were on the other side of the River, or the gods of the Amorites, in whose land you dwell. But as for me and my house, we will serve the Lord" (Joshua 24:15).

Joshua confirmed this word by establishing a rock of remembrance, about which he declared to all the people: "Behold this stone shall be a witness to us, for it has heard all the words of the Lord which He spoke to us. It shall therefore be a witness to you, lest you deny your God" (Joshua 24:26–27).

Resting in the front flowerbed of our home in California is a large rock over which I have spoken these same words. Inspired by a message from my pastor, Jack Hayford, I stood before that rock and declared aloud, "As for me and my house, we will serve the Lord."

Contemplating this commitment, I realized how essential prayer is to the one God has appointed to serve as head of a household. An absence of prayer from the head will ultimately diminish that person's capacity to make wise decisions, and the whole family will suffer.

Later I read the psalmist's words often quoted when new church buildings are being erected: "Unless the Lord builds the house, they labor in vain who build it" (Psalm 127:1). The context of this psalm deals with the family. Subsequent verses declare, "Behold, children are a heritage from the Lord, the fruit of the womb is His reward, like arrows in the hand of a warrior, so are the children of one's youth" (Psalm 127:3–4). Quite simply, when the psalmist speaks of building a house, he is describing the establishing of a healthy household.

Other biblical injunctions likewise focus on the spiritual well-being of the family. Concerning lessons Israel learned in their wilderness wanderings, Moses declared: "Only take heed to yourself, and diligently keep yourself, lest you forget the things your eyes have seen, and lest they depart from your heart all the days of your life. And teach them to your children and your grandchildren" (Deuteronomy 4:9). The author of Proverbs advises, "Train up a child in the way he should go, and when he is old he will not depart from it" (Proverbs 22:6). Surely prayer ought to be at the heart of showing a child the right path.

To the Ephesians, Paul would later write: "And now a word to you parents. Don't keep on scolding and nagging your children, making them angry and resentful. Rather, bring them up with the loving discipline the Lord Himself approves, with suggestions and godly advice" (Ephesians 6:4, LB). Interestingly, these words on family health immediately precede Scripture's most in-depth analysis of spiritual warfare (Ephesians 6:10–18)!

Because prayer is so essential to communicating godly advice and loving discipline, let us look more closely at several suggestions for developing a praying family.

Praying in the Family

"Like father, like son" is an adage that speaks volumes when it comes to prayer. Are our children learning the importance of prayer *by our example?*

Consider the example of Abraham (Genesis 18:16–22). Here the patriarch speaks with angels who reveal their mission to destroy Sodom and Gomorrah because of sin in the cities. The passage reads:

> Then the men rose from there and looked toward Sodom, and Abraham went with them to send them on the way. And the Lord said, "Shall I hide from Abraham what I am doing, since Abraham shall surely become a great and mighty nation, and all the nations of the earth shall be blessed in him? For I have known him, in order that he may command his children and his household after him,

that they keep the way of the Lord, and do righteousness and justice, that the Lord may bring to Abraham what He has spoken to him."

(Genesis 18:16–19)

The Lord's confidence in Abraham's ability to administrate his household is revealed in the words "For I have known him. . . ." Abraham set an example of one who sought God. Time and again we see Abraham erecting altars to the Lord as focal points for worship.

Do our children see this quality in us? If not, the following suggestions may be helpful.

First, *create a climate of prayer at home*. This begins by communicating with your family the importance of prayer. During our daughters' early years, they would always see Dee reading her Bible when they arrived at the breakfast table. A small thing, perhaps, but vital. It demonstrated the importance of spiritual nourishment.

We should also bring prayer into family activities, such as when going on trips or planning family activities. Prayer is appropriate during times of discipline. When disciplining either of our daughters in their early years, I always assured her that the punishment was not because I didn't love her. Then I would hold the child tightly as we prayed a short prayer of tender dependence on the Holy Spirit to help us live better.

Second, *create a place of prayer in the home*. I call such a place at our family home the "Gap," based on God's message in Ezekiel's day: "I sought for a man among them that should make up the hedge, and stand in the gap before me for the land, that I should not destroy it; but I found none" (Ezekiel 22:30, KJV).

A "Gap" is a place for devotions and family prayers. It

might be located in a large closet, unused room, even a shed in the backyard. Our own family Gap began with a small aluminum shed less than ten feet square. The entire cost, with wood paneling, carpet, and electrical heating, was far less than many families spend on recreation and incidentals for a few months in a year.

A family Gap should minister to the entire family. You might want to buy devotional books suitable for family members of different ages. An inexpensive bulletin board can feature prayer requests from missionaries or evangelism ministries like Every Home for Christ. EHC's World Prayer Map would be especially helpful. (See page 188 for information on the availability of such helpful prayer tools.) A map of the world attached to a wall can give an increased global atmosphere. A trip to a travel agent might yield colorful posters of exotic places.

Be creative in your planning and the result will be a special place of prayer.

Third, *create a program of prayer in the home.* Ask the Holy Spirit to show you a simple plan for developing a daily prayer strategy that you might apply for use with your family. For example, you might want to adopt the seven prayer focuses (one for each day of the week), as outlined in the immediately preceding chapters of this book. With a little creativity, all seven of these focuses, including the family focus, can be adapted to any age group.

Praying for Your Family

Two Scripture passages provide patterns for daily prayer in families. One is from the Old Testament account of King David, while the other is from the New Testament account of our King of kings, Jesus Christ.

In David's prayer for forgiveness we find our first pattern: "Create in me a clean heart, O God, and renew a steadfast spirit within me. Do not cast me away from Your presence, and do not take Your Holy Spirit from me" (Psalm 51:10–11).

Our second pattern emerges from Luke's New Testament description of the early growth years of our Lord. Luke wrote: "And Jesus increased in wisdom and stature, and in favor with God and men" (Luke 2:52).

As our children were growing up I often employed these two passages in daily prayer as a reminder of our family's spiritual and material needs. I would start by asking for a clean heart, following David's plea. Then I would pray for a spirit of purity to permeate my entire family. Next, I would ask the Lord to renew a "steadfast spirit" within me, transferring that quality, too, to the entire household. I would claim a special measure of God's presence for each member of our family as we moved into the day's activities. (Of course, I was praying more for a *recognition* of His presence than for Him to do something He was reluctant to do. God is with us whether we realize it or not, but acknowledging our dependence on Him often leads to blessings we might not otherwise experience.) And finally, I would pray with David, "Take not Your Holy Spirit from me," claiming a special portion of the Holy Spirit in each of us so that we might live a life pleasing to Jesus.

In thinking of Luke's description of Christ's early years, a meaningful fourfold pattern of prayer for our children emerged.

First, I prayed for our children's *spiritual growth.* Luke spoke of Jesus increasing "in favor with God," a reference to our Lord's spiritual growth patterns. Although born without sin, Jesus still had to spend time in prayer and study of Scriptures. Years later, He would confront Satan in the wilderness quoting just the right Scripture for each temptation. This was not because Jesus was programmed from eternity to know the Scriptures, but because He studied the Scriptures as a youth. Remember, when Christ lived on earth, He was a man subjected to all the struggles each of us must face and He had to be mature spiritually to face these temptations without sin.

Second, I prayed for our children's *physical growth.* Jesus not only grew in favor with God but "in stature." This focus allowed me to concentrate a moment's prayer on the physical development of my family, including healthy eating habits and a wise maintenance of our physical "temples." My regular trips to the tennis courts with our daughters in their pre-teen years was but one outflow of this prayer. It led to both girls excelling in four years of high school tennis. During this physical growth focus I would also claim physical health for each of our girls in turn.

Third, I prayed for their *mental growth.* Luke tells us that Jesus increased in wisdom. I petitioned God to help our daughters develop wise stewardship of their mental abilities. I prayed for their grades in school and that God would guide them in their choice of subjects best suited to the field of service to which He would ultimately lead them.

Finally, I prayed for the girls' *social growth.* When the Bible tells us Jesus increased in favor with men, it meant He had gained the respect of those about Him. He was not a social outcast. He was the essence of spirituality but was never religiously obnoxious. Based on Christ's example, I prayed that God would give our children good balance in their social relationships. I also prayed for the friends our daughters would select, and for the girls' ability to discern unhealthy friendships.

As I developed these simple prayer patterns, I was repeatedly reminded that there is no greater gift a parent (or a grandparent or grandchild) can give a child than the covering of prayer. As the noted Norwegian Bible teacher Professor Halesby said: "My friend, if you are not able to leave your children a legacy in the form of goods, do not worry. And do not worry yourself to death either physically or spiritually in order to accumulate a great deal of property for your children. But see to it, night and day, that you pray for them. Then you will leave them a great legacy of answers to prayer, which will follow them all the days of their lives."

Praying as a Family

Christ spoke of the significance of small group prayer: "I say to you that if two of you agree on earth concerning anything that they ask, it will be done for them by My Father in heaven. For where two or three are gathered together in My name, I am there in the midst of them" (Matthew 18:19–20).

Perhaps the most natural of all small prayer groups is the family. Where else do we have an equal opportunity for an ongoing small corporate prayer gathering that can meet on a daily basis?

But to do this in a meaningful way we need a basic plan. Here is a family prayer pattern you may find helpful:

First begin with *a worship focus.* Worship is at the heart of a healthy prayer experience. Worship includes all aspects of prayer that focus on God's nature and character. Praise, thanksgiving, and even singing might be included here. (Please see the author's book *A Celebration of Praise*, Baker Book House, 1984, for suggestions to help you get off to a good start in your time of praise and worship.)

Secondly, include a *Word focus*. Paul told Timothy, ". . . From childhood you have known the Holy Scriptures, which are able to make you wise for salvation through faith which is in Christ Jesus" (2 Timothy 3:15). Someone took time to plant God's Word in Timothy's heart while he was still very young. Consider Paul's words to young Timothy: "I thank God . . . when I call to remembrance the genuine faith that is in you, which dwelt first in your grandmother Lois and your mother Eunice . . ." (2 Timothy 1:3, 5). It appears that it was young Timothy's mother and grandmother who taught this future warrior God's Word.

One never knows when planting Scripture in the heart of a child the extent to which God might someday use those seeds to change nations.

You may wish to use a classic devotional guide such as *Streams in the Desert* or *My Utmost for His Highest*. For younger children you can use such books as *Hurlbut's Story of the Bible* or *Egermeier's Bible Story Book*. Another possible plan is the author's systematic study of God's Word as presented in the book *The University of the Word* (Regal Books, 1983). Because twelve different biblical principles are emphasized in this study, the concepts can become a twelve-month family devotional focus. Each month a different spiritual growth principle would be the focus.

Third, following your important worship and Word focuses, conclude with a *world focus*, interceding for a lost and needy world. You might wish to follow an Acts 1:8

pattern, which speaks of believers receiving power after they have been touched by God's Spirit. As a result, they become witnesses for Jesus in "Jerusalem . . . Judaea, and in Samaria, and unto the uttermost part of the earth"(Acts 1:8, KJV).

Here we find an excellent threefold plan of prayer for family altar. First, *we pray for our Jerusalem.* This concerns local needs, such as our community. Second, *we pray for our Judaea and Samaria.* This involves our state (or, in some countries, our province) and our nation. Third, *we pray for the uttermost parts of the earth* that include unevangelized nations never reached completely with the Gospel.

thirteen
Soul Conflict
Taking Authority Against
Spiritual Darkness

In the last chapter I spoke about a family's intercessory headquarters which I call the Gap—in our case the little shed in our backyard dedicated to prayer. The idea of the Gap as a place for personal and family intercession came into being in the latter part of the 1960s during the hippie movement.

There was a very real danger that the youth of our own church would be swept into such lifestyles, and I was concerned. They were seriously at risk unless they were taught the importance of prayer.

So I began planning weekend prayer retreats into the nearby Sierra Nevada Mountains, specifically for the teenagers of our church. The first retreat included 22 participants. We were all inexperienced in prolonged prayer sessions. Not one of us, for instance, knew how to pray an entire night, and frankly we were all about to give up after less than an hour.

Then the youngest participant, a thirteen-year-old, asked us to start praying in a different way—as warriors. He saw himself and his friends as warring against the darkness of the booze-sex-drugs lifestyle of the hippie communes, and he asked us to stand with him all night to "fight the devil." This youth had tears in his eyes as he spoke, and all agreed to go to war along with him.

By three in the morning a spirit of brokenness had settled over our retreat house. The room was warmly lit by a glow from logs burning in a large fireplace, but also from a fire burning within the young people themselves. We all began to weep and cry out. One seventeen-year-old student lay on her face in the middle of the room weeping for the youth of California who were in trouble with drugs.

I was witnessing what our forebears used to call a "spirit of travail," a wonderful word related to the word *work* or *labor*, as in giving birth.

And indeed, the intercessory retreats from our church flourished, until 175 young people were participating. Within a year the Jesus Movement began in many parts of California. At least 800,000 young people would find Christ in those same exciting days.

And amid all this, something profound was happening in my own life. God was placing in my heart a yearning for more of Himself, a hunger that was to explode on a life-changing Wednesday night in 1971.

On that evening I arrived at church an hour-and-a-half before our regular midweek youth intercessory prayer meeting. I made my way to a secluded storage area behind the platform of our church where I often went to find a quiet place to pray. Hidden away amid the boxes of costumes and props for Christmas and Easter pageants, I began to seek the Lord for an outpouring of His Spirit upon the youth of our church.

At first nothing out of the ordinary happened. Then, without much forethought, I asked God a simple, direct question. Hearing His voice in my heart was an entirely new experience, but that night I found I was expecting an answer.

"What do you want me to do with my life?" I asked the Lord.

Suddenly I heard the most startling answer. The words were surprisingly clear: *Because you have asked me this night, I will tell you this night.*

I had never heard the Lord speak so clearly. Tears began to flow as I waited for what was to follow.

The answer came not as a voice but a picture, alive with movement. I saw an army of God's people marching. It was a remarkable sight. The army, six to eight abreast, stretched as far as the eye could see. It formed a vast column that seemed to continue forever.

"Who are these people, Lord," I cried, "and where are they going?"

A quiet answer followed: *This is an army of intercessors who will change the world. I'm calling you to help mobilize this army.*

Before I could respond the picture changed. I was looking at a large white-frame mansion. Coming and going from the building were clean-cut young people carrying Bibles, unusual in a day when communes were everywhere and long-haired youths living together was common.

These are residents at a house of prayer, the Lord told me. Each young person had made a commitment to give a significant "time gift" for intercessory prayer. Some were there for a summer, most for an entire year.

Then the Lord took me inside the building. A large sign was attached to the door on my right at the entrance. The sign was hand-painted, as if by one of the young people, and it quoted a portion of Ezekiel: "I sought for a man among them, that should make up the hedge and stand in the gap before me for the land . . ." (Ezekiel 22:30, KJV). Just above the Scripture were the words *The Gap*.

The door opened slowly. Looking inside this room designated the Gap I saw a young lady, perhaps nineteen years of age. She had long brown hair and silver-rimmed glasses and she was kneeling at a small, round table upon which rested a globe. As I watched, she lifted the globe a few inches off the table and began to weep.

Then a young man came into the Gap and the girl transferred her burden to him. After a while he, too, passed the globe to another. This continued as I watched in silence.

"Lord, this is beautiful," I said softly.

He responded with the challenge, *I want you to bring into being exactly what you have seen here.*

The vision was over. There, in the storage room behind the platform of our church, I heard our own young people beginning to arrive for the evening.

That night I shared the vision with our youth. There was unusual excitement and the young people assured me they were ready to help bring my vision to life. I knew that night that God wanted me to find the white-frame building and transform it into a prayer center.

Within six months God did give us our first "house of prayer" in Sacramento, California. Within five years God gave me one hundred young people, each committed to a year of intercession. They supported themselves by "praying in" the finances to help us continue our ministry. Out of those 50,000 continuous hours of prayer, day and night, including holidays, God gave birth to prayer training that ultimately touched over a million believers in more than 120 countries of the world.

It all began when a hundred young people made themselves available for a year of prayer. Later, when asked how my prayer ministry began, I could say, "It started with a century's worth of prayer." One hundred youths sanctifying a year of their lives equalled a century's worth of prayer commitment.

Changing Our World

A second life-changing vision occurred nine years later. By that time the first vision had become a reality. God had given us our prayer center and thousands of additional Gap Ministries had sprung up in houses and churches throughout the world, often in unusual circumstances. A Lutheran day school teacher built a Gap shaped like Noah's ark. There her pre-school children went for as long as thirty minutes a day of prayer. It was often difficult to get the children to stop praying. They had discovered prayer can be fun.

Years later I visited a church in Malaysia that had grown to nearly 5,000 members in less than eight years. This church, thriving in a land where the law prohibits witnessing to a Muslim, had a center where intercessors came for days of concentrated prayer. When entering the center I noticed each door leading to a private prayer room had a Gap sign similar to the one I had first seen in my vision.

Later I learned that a brother from New Zealand was sharing our vision everywhere. He had passed through the region several years earlier.

As the years passed and the army began to increase, God opened the doors for me to take this prayer vision to many nations through the ministry of World Literature Crusade, now Every Home for Christ. The founder, Dr. Jack McAlister, having heard of our prayer ministry and believing prayer to be essential to the ultimate evangelization of the world, asked me to join his staff to develop prayer training for believers of all denominations.

Not realizing I would someday serve Every Home for Christ as their international president, I joined the ministry and developed the Change the World School of Prayer. The School of Prayer was (and continues to be) a training course designed to strengthen believers in their daily devotional habits and to equip them to pray effectively for world evangelization. One important aspect of the training is the challenge for believers to consider giving God a gift of one hour daily for personal prayer. Based on Christ's challenge to His disciples, "Could you not watch one hour?" more than 200,000 Christians have made the commitment. Thousands more have agreed to invest fifteen or thirty minutes a day.

But as the army began to grow, I became increasingly concerned about focusing all this prayer energy on what would bring Christ the most glory. Prayer, after all, is not given as a means to gain increased material or spiritual pleasure, though personal blessings do result from a healthy prayer experience. Rather, prayer is God's supreme gift to assist the Church in establishing His Kingdom throughout the earth.

As I continued my search of the Scriptures concerning

the importance of prayer, I became convinced that believers are engaged in spiritual war that must be waged on biblical principles. Just as Satan has an established order in the invisible realm, so believers must develop a strategy to stand effectively against these forces. The more I traveled, the more convinced I became that every region of the world has a controlling spirit ruling over it. It became evident that something must be developed to restrain these forces.

Which is the background to the second major vision experience of my life. It occurred following several days of fasting and prayer during a trip to Michigan. My devotional time in my motel room beside Lake Michigan began much like that of any other day. I had come to the final chapters of the book of Revelation in my daily Bible reading, and pausing to meditate on the literal nature of the Lamb's Book of Life, I suddenly found myself longing to pray about names *yet to be added* to this most unusual of celestial records. And I blurted out a most unusual prayer.

"Lord," I prayed, "please let me participate in a movement that adds more names to the Book of Life than have been added in all of history."

It was a bold prayer, indeed, but somehow I felt the Holy Spirit had led me to say the words. Tears began to flow as I stood up and walked to the window of my motel room. Before me was the vast expanse of Lake Michigan lying placidly like a giant sheet of glass. As the sun's rays sparkled off the lake, I saw millions of tiny diamond-like bursts of light dancing in the distance. It reminded me of the description in Revelation of the multitude of redeemed humanity who will someday stand upon a sea of glass (Revelation 15:2). Then I recalled the promise of how "blood-washed" souls would come out of every kindred, tongue, people, and nation (Revelation 5:9). I was convinced God had appointed the moment to reveal to me the role of intercessors in global evangelism.

Lifting my face in anticipation, I experienced the second vision that would impact my ministry so strongly.

Before me, in a large arena, stood a multitude representing every age group. I sensed that all these people in the arena were committed intercessors. Each held a page containing names.

I wondered what these names represented, and why everyone in the massive gathering of believers had a personal list.

Suddenly my attention was drawn in the opposite direction. There I saw a throne and an angel who held a huge book. As I watched, each intercessor came to the throne and presented his list of names.

One individual caught my particular attention. She was well beyond seventy years of age. But although her face was wrinkled and her hair gray, she beamed with the joy of Jesus.

Soon she, too, was standing before the angel presenting her list of names. As the angel began recording the names in the great Book, I asked the Lord what all this meant.

"These are the names of souls these warriors helped bring to a knowledge of My salvation."

"Where did the intercessors get these names?" I prayed.

"Come, and I will show you," came the answer.

With that I saw this elderly saint, on her knees, flying swiftly through the heavenlies. It was a strange sight. In my spirit I knew she was entering a level of warfare I had never seen, and that she was flying thousands of miles. In an instant, she descended to hover over a village that seemed to me to be in India, although I had never been there. My attention was drawn to a hut that appeared to be the focus of the saint's intercession.

The hut was modest, even by the standards of the village. Within were a small table, a chair, and a bed. Its lone occupant was a middle-aged man who appeared to be of Indian descent, most likely a Hindu.

As the intercessor continued in prayer above the hut, I noticed that even with the sun shining brightly, the hut was dark.

Then I noticed movement in the village. A man was distributing Gospel literature. He paused at the hut and knocked gently. When the occupant opened the door the worker handed him a Gospel booklet.

Through all this the elderly saint remained stationary in the heavenlies as if waiting for something.

Closing the door, the Hindu read a few sentences that told him about a loving heavenly Father who came to earth in the form of a man, God's only Son, a concept beyond the Hindu's comprehension. He believed there were many gods, perhaps millions. A monkey could be a god, or a cow or snake. Even a tree might be an object of worship. "One God, one Son," he thought. "Nonsense." He tossed the book on the table. It seemed the darkness of the room prevented his comprehension of the truth.

The man's rejection of the message seemed to be the cue the intercessor was waiting for. Into the darkness she plunged, through the roof of the hut, landing on her knees. The Hindu had no idea she was there.

Reaching her hands forward along the floor, with her palms up, the elderly woman appeared to be lifting something. Then I realized what she was doing. She was lifting the darkness in the room! The more she prayed, the more the darkness moved. When she had raised it high enough, she slowly moved from her knees and began pushing the darkness toward the ceiling from a crouched position, a few inches at a time, as she continued her intercession. Before long she had pushed the darkness above the man and was standing stretched to her capacity, warring all the while against the satanic darkness.

The instant the darkness rose above the man's head, he turned again toward the table, gazing intently upon the message he had earlier rejected. Now there was a different look on his face, a look of longing.

He walked to the table and took the booklet into his hand. I could hear his thoughts as he slowly read the opening sentences a second time. "Perhaps I was hasty in rejecting this message," he reasoned. As he read again the claims of Christ, an amazing thing happened. He lifted his face toward heaven, his unseen praying guest contending against the darkness beside him, and he cried out to the Lord, "I believe You are the Son of God!"

Joy flooded the faces of both the new convert and the elderly intercessor. A miracle was happening before my eyes. In that instant a brilliant beam of light penetrated the hut and flowed into the heart of the new believer. He had seen the Light—literally. All darkness in the room vanished. The intercessor's work, at least for the moment, had ended.

Still unseen by the rejoicing Indian, the intercessor stepped from the hut and pulled a piece of paper from her pocket. I recognized it immediately. It was the list she had presented to the angel with the Book. The happy warrior added the man's name to her long list. Then, with a shout of praise, she tucked the list back into her pocket and headed for a hut across the way.

For the next several minutes I sat wondering quietly

about the strange picture I had just witnessed. Had my imagination run wild or had I truly observed an intercessor in action? God's Word would hold my answer. Any vision must find confirmation in God's Word.

Almost immediately I began to recall confirming passages regarding the power of God's light to penetrate the darkness:

> Arise, shine, for your light has come, and the glory of the Lord rises upon you. See . . . thick darkness is over the peoples, but the Lord rises upon you and his glory appears over you. Nations will come to your light, and kings to the brightness of your dawn. Lift up your eyes and look about you: All assemble and come to you; your sons come from afar, and your daughters are carried on the arm. Then you will look and be radiant, your heart will throb and swell with joy; the wealth on the seas will be brought to you, to you the riches of the nations will come.
>
> (Isaiah 60:1–5, NIV)

Other confirming passages followed. As I evaluated these biblical insights, four facts regarding the intercessor's conflict with the darkness on behalf of lost souls emerged.

The Desire of the Lord

Fact one: *It is the Lord's desire to see every person on earth provided access to the Gospel of Jesus Christ.*

This reality is stated throughout the New Testament. Peter wrote, "The Lord is not slack concerning His promise, as some count slackness, but is longsuffering toward us, not willing that any should perish but that all should come to repentance" (2 Peter 3:9). *The Living Bible* renders it: "The Lord isn't really being slow about his promised return, even though it sometimes seems that way. But he is waiting, for the good reason that he is not willing that any should perish, and he is giving more time for sinners to repent."

Of particular interest is the paraphrase of verse 15: "And remember why He is waiting. He is giving us time to get His message of salvation out to others."

Other passages likewise share the importance of "all the world" and "every creature" (Mark 16:15) having access to the Gospel. When Christ discussed end-time events with His disciples, He clearly expressed that total fulfillment of the Great Commission was essential to the wrap-up of this present age. Mark records these words of Christ: "And the gospel must first be preached to all the nations" (Mark 13:10). Matthew includes the promise, "And this gospel of the kingdom will be preached in all the world as a witness to all the nations, and then the end will come" (Matthew 24:14).

Paul later spoke of the harvest, in a context of prayer. To young Timothy he wrote, "Therefore I exhort first of all that supplications, prayers, intercessions, and giving of thanks be made for all men, for kings and all who are in authority, that we may lead a quiet and peaceable life in all godliness and reverence" (1 Timothy 2:1–2). Paul then adds the important ultimate result of these prayers: "For this is good and acceptable in the sight of God our Savior, who desires all men to be saved and to come to the knowledge of the truth" (verses 3–4).

The message is clear. God desires all to have access to

the Gospel, and prayer is at the heart of making that possible. But a second fact is necessary to understand if we're to pursue prayer to its greatest potential.

The Plan of the Enemy

Fact two: *It is Satan's plan to prevent every unbeliever from receiving access to the Gospel of Jesus Christ.* On the surface, this is common sense. Yet we often fail to understand that lost souls, whether family members or unevangelized people groups overseas, are covered with a spiritual darkness they have not, in fact, chosen. True, they are responsible for their sins and cannot be redeemed if they reject salvation, but they did not choose to be born in sin.

Paul instructs Timothy to preach the Gospel so that unbelievers will "come to their senses and escape from the devil's snare, in which they have been caught and held at [Satan's] will" (2 Timothy 2:25–26, NEB).

Satan holds unbelievers in his total control. They are "held at his will" and, according to Ephesians 2:1–2, *Amplified Bible,* "under his control." The unbeliever's darkened spiritual condition is such that until that darkness is removed he cannot see the light. Thus, darkness must be dealt with at a supernatural level if the person is to break through into the brightness of Christ's eternal light.

The more I contemplated this concept, following my vision of the elderly intercessor and the Hindu, the more I wondered if any specific Scripture expressly said such. To my amazement, in my next day's systematic Bible reading I discovered a passage I had read many times before, but had never seen its significance in the context of warring against the darkness on behalf of lost souls.

It was found in Paul's second letter to the Corinthians:

> But even if our gospel is veiled [hidden], it is veiled to those who are perishing, whose minds the god of this age has blinded, who do not believe, lest the light of the gospel of the glory of Christ, who is the image of God, should shine on them.
>
> (2 Corinthians 4:3–4)

Note the paraphrase of this passage: "If the Good News we preach is hidden to anyone, it is hidden from the one who is on the road to eternal death. Satan, who is the god of this evil world, has made him blind, unable to see the glorious light of the Gospel that is shining upon him, or to understand the amazing message we preach about the glory of Christ, who is God" (TLB).

The implication in this passage is clear. Remove the darkness and the light will shine. Yet the one covered with darkness is incapable of removing this darkness on his own.

Further, when a person first receives the Gospel, our enemy immediately attempts to snatch the seed away (see Mark 4:14–15). Do seeds finally take root because an intercessor stands against the enemy, preventing the seed from being snatched away?

This question is vital because the harvest depends on the seed's taking root. Which brings us to fact number three:

The Duty of the Church

Fact Three: *It is the Church's duty to take the Gospel of Jesus Christ to every person on earth.*

Here again is a biblical concept readily accepted by most mature believers. And yet most Christians lack any systematic involvement in communicating the Gospel, whether here or overseas. This, I believe, will soon change radically.

Note again Matthew's familiar record of Christ's words:

"All authority has been given to Me in heaven and on earth. Go therefore and make disciples of all the nations, baptizing them in the name of the Father and of the Son and of the Holy Spirit, teaching them to observe all things that I have commanded you. . . ."

(Matthew 28:18–20)

Mark's rendering reads:

"Go into all the world and preach the gospel to every creature."

(Mark 16:15)

Even Old Testament passages prophesied the fulfillment of the Great Commission. Of the Messiah, the psalmist wrote: "Yes, all kings shall fall down before Him; all nations shall serve Him. His name shall endure forever; His name shall continue as long as the sun; and men shall be blessed in Him; all nations shall call Him blessed" (Psalm 72:11, 17). Isaiah said simply, "For the earth shall be full of the knowledge of the Lord as the waters cover the sea" (Isaiah 11:9).

The Church has a duty to take Christ's love to every dark heart on planet earth. And it is here that the intercessor's work becomes absolutely essential.

The Role of the Intercessor

Fact Four: *It is the intercessor's responsibility to hold back the unseen forces of satanic darkness wherever the Gospel of Jesus Christ is shared.*

We know by Scripture that although human beings occupy a physical plane, their actions and activities are controlled from the invisible realm. All warfare for a soul takes place in that same unseen arena. Recall Paul's warfare words to the Ephesian believers that we wrestle "against . . . [the master spirits who are] the world rulers of this present darkness, against the spirit forces of wickedness in the heavenly, (supernatural) sphere" (Ephesians 6:10, 12, AMPLIFIED).

It is because of Paul's awareness of spiritual warfare that he pleaded with the churches repeatedly to remember him in prayer, as he did the Thessalonians: "Finally, brothers, pray for us that the message of the Lord may spread rapidly and be honored, just as it was with you. And pray that we may be delivered from wicked and evil men, for not everyone has faith" (2 Thessalonians 3:1–2, NIV).

In equally strong terms Paul wrote the Romans: "Now I beg you, brethren, through the Lord Jesus Christ, and through the love of the Spirit, that you strive together with me in your prayers to God for me" (Romans 15:30). Paul was convinced that his ministry could go no further than the prayers of his fellow warriors would allow.

The intercessor has a vital role to play in helping unbelievers "come to their senses and escape the snare of the devil." (2 Timothy 2:25–26). And the more I thought about these Bible-based facts, the more convinced I became that intercessors who contend for lost souls do indeed help add names to the Lamb's Book of Life. They may not be aware that they are sweeping through the heavenlies on their knees, or that they are contending against the darkness for a soul who has just been confronted with the claims of Christ, but their prayers make the harvest possible.

The Vision Confirmed

Six years following my unusual vision of the elderly intercessor and her global prayer mission, God confirmed the validity of the vision in an unusual way.

It happened when I made my first trip to India. There I visited all the major regions of that vast and complex land. As I traveled through the countryside I was overwhelmed by the many huts that looked exactly like the hut I first observed in my prayer time six years earlier.

Departing India with a most unusual burden for these masses, I headed home. Somewhere over the vast expanse of the Pacific I picked up a challenging book I'd been given in Calcutta, Paul Pillai's book *India's Search for the Unknown Christ*. Unexpectedly, when I came to page 212, I couldn't keep back the tears. The author told of a Hindu leader in the Arya Samag sect who lived many years ago in the region of Rajasthan. He was an angry man consumed with a passion to fight all Christian work. More than once he had stopped young Christians who were witnessing and removed their Bibles and publicly burned them.

On one such occasion Paul Pillai himself had been part of a team who encountered this hostility. They had been going house-to-house and standing on street corners distributing small Gospels of John.

Suddenly the angry man appeared and demanded their Gospel booklets. Keeping only one, perhaps as evidence, he set the remainder on fire. Then he threatened to kill anyone on the team who continued witnessing for Jesus. The man left the scene angrily with his evidence in hand, a lone copy of John's Gospel.

Three weeks later Paul Pillai received a letter from that same man. He wrote that he had taken the Gospel of John home with him and after reading a few pages tossed it on the table in his hut, convinced it was filled with lies. But that night, in the blackness of the evening, he felt a strange presence enter the room. The man couldn't get his mind off the booklet on the table. Finally he stood and made his way in darkness toward the table.

As he picked up the booklet that second time, a supernatural light illumined the room. He looked down at the booklet and read: "He that believeth on him is not condemned: but he that believeth not is condemned already, because he hath not believed in the name of the only begotten Son of God. And this is the condemnation, that light is come into the world, and men loved darkness rather than light, because their deeds were evil. For every one that doeth evil hateth the light, neither cometh to the light . . ." (John 3:18–20, KJV).

In that instant he knelt down and received Christ as Savior. He declared later that in his search for truth, his eyes had been blinded by his own preconceived images.

Although my vision of six years earlier had several differences with the story I read, I was overwhelmed by the similarities. Had the unusual presence in the Hindu man's room been the working of the Holy Spirit in response to an intercessor's prayers? Or had the intercessor actually been there, in spirit, as the result of the operation of the Holy Spirit released through that intercessor's prayers?

I had no answers. But I became convinced that prayer plays a vital role in the conflict for a soul. It had happened with me. True, by an act of my own will, I had chosen to believe. But somewhere, somehow, an intercessor confronted the darkness on my behalf. In my case I know the identity of the intercessor. It was my mother. She loved me on her knees. Her intercession drove away the darkness so that the light of Christ might penetrate my heart during days of youthful rebellion.

Beloved intercessor, the world is waiting for your love. I invite you to be a praying participant today in seeing names added to that glorious celestial record John describes in Revelation. Our final chapter will tell you how you can be involved in the greatest harvest in the history of the church—if we will pray.

fourteen
Prayer Travelers
Mobilizing a Movement of World Prayer Missionaries

The gifted writer S. D. Gordon said, "The real victory in all service is won beforehand in prayer. Service is merely gathering up the results." Expanding on this thought as related to the Great Commission, W. Stanley Mooneyham adds, "Let us stop complaining that we don't have enough people, enough money, enough tools. That simply is not true. There is no shortage of anything we need—except of vision and prayer and will. Prayer is the one resource immediately available to us all. If more Christians were on their knees praying, more Christians would be on their feet evangelizing."

The missionary leader continues, "Robert Speer, a great Presbyterian missions pioneer and leader, wrote: 'The evangelization of the world depends first upon a revival of prayer. Deeper than the need for workers; deeper, far, than the need for money; deep down at the bottom of our spiritual lives, is the need for the forgotten secret of prevailing, worldwide prayer. Missions have progressed slowly abroad because piety and prayer have been shallow at home.' "

A Call for World Prayer Missionaries

The vision that came to me in 1971, of the elderly saint warring against darkness, was the stimulus for a highly focused work that we call World Prayer Missionaries.

Simply stated, a World Prayer Missionary is any follower of Jesus who will go daily in prayer to a specific region of the world to engage in a carefully planned strategy of spiritual warfare.

The World Prayer Missionary selects a specific country, a region or province of that country, and even a base city when possible. Just as a conventional missionary must determine what country God wants him to evangelize, and what city in that country to live in, the World Prayer Missionary must define his or her specific focuses carefully for prayer. And just as a conventional missionary must seek God for an evangelism strategy regarding his or her area of responsibility, the World Prayer Missionary must seek the Holy Spirit for a specific prayer strategy regarding his area of prayer focus.

A Bible Basis for the World Prayer Missionary

From a biblical standpoint the World Prayer Missionary has a fourfold function:

First, *the World Prayer Missionary is a forerunner*. Isaiah wrote: "For Zion's sake I will not hold My peace, and for Jerusalem's sake I will not rest, until her righteousness goes forth as brightness, and her salvation as a lamp that burns. The Gentiles shall see your righteousness, and all kings your glory . . ." (Isaiah 62:1–2).

The prophet continues, "Go through, go through the gates! Prepare the way for the people; build up, build up the highway! Take out the stones, lift up a banner for the peoples!" (Isaiah 62:10).

Isaiah speaks here of a forerunner, an individual who helps prepare the way for others to follow. The World Prayer Missionary serves this function. He or she goes into spiritual warfare long before conventional workers enter the conflict. Because the obstacles that hinder evangelism originate in the unseen realm, we must deal with them in this same realm. Thus, the World Prayer Missionary enters the conflict in advance of the missionary or Christian worker. He or she goes to places that even missionaries cannot go.

Second, *the World Prayer Missionary is himself or herself an actual, spiritual war club.* A World Prayer Missionary actually becomes a weapon in God's hands. The prophet Isaiah referred to God's watchmen as "a crown of glory in the hand of the Lord, and a royal diadem in the hand of your God" (Isaiah 62:3). Note God's description of King Cyrus: "You are My battle-ax and weapon of war: for with you I will break the nation in pieces; with you I will destroy kingdoms; with you I will break in pieces the horse and its rider" (Jeremiah 51:20–21). *The New International Version* says of Cyrus, "You are my war club."

True, this passage is speaking of an earthly king, Cyrus, and not specifically of intercessors. Still, it reminds us that in every generation God will raise up His people to carry out His purposes.

Third, *the World Prayer Missionary is a threshing sledge.*

Here we find a most unique description of one who is called to the ministry of destroying Satan's works through prayer. Isaiah wrote, "Behold, I will make you into a new threshing sledge with sharp teeth; you shall thresh the mountains and beat them small, and make the hills like chaff" (Isaiah 41:15).

When Isaiah spoke of a "threshing sledge" he employed the Hebrew word *mowrag,* meaning to pulverize completely, or to crush and grind at the same time. The teeth of the sledge are both new and sharp. They are capable of pulverizing all that Satan would raise up to block God's plan.

This is the work of the World Prayer Missionary. He or she selects a region of the world, identifies opposing spiritual forces in that region, and through prayer pulverizes them completely.

Fourth, *the World Prayer Missionary is a ruling authority.* Through Jeremiah God declared, "See, I have this day set you over the nations and over the kingdoms, to root out and to pull down, to destroy and to throw down, to build and to plant" (Jeremiah 1:10).

The World Prayer Missionary is a ruler. In prayer, under the full authority and supervision of Jesus Christ, the Head of the Church, he or she rules over geographic regions of the earth.

Qualifications

Note these words of Christ to His disciples: "Have faith in God. For assuredly, I say to you, whoever says to this mountain, 'Be removed and be cast into the sea,' and does not doubt in his heart, but believes that those things he says will come to pass, he will have whatever he says" (Mark 11:22–23).

An evaluation of this passage reveals three qualifications regarding candidates for the office of a World Prayer Missionary.

First is the *eligibility factor*. Note the words *Whoever says to this mountain*. Any believer in right standing with the Lord is eligible to be a mountain-mover. No matter what a person's gifts or abilities, the willing warrior is qualified to be a World Prayer Missionary. Availability is the key. It is as if the Lord is saying, "Give Me a believer who is available, and I can work out all the details necessary to give that person the strength to fulfill any task to which I might call him."

Second is the *authority factor*. In Mark 11:22–23 Jesus pictures a confident disciple taking direct authority against an inanimate object. A confident intercessor is convinced of his position in Christ and puts his conviction into words. Power is released not so much by his faith as by the declaration of his lips expressing that faith.

Finally is the *certainty factor*. Here we see Christ's emphasis on our need for absolute assurance that He will carry out what we command with our lips, providing our commands measure up to His will. He says, "Whosoever says . . . and does not doubt . . ." (Mark 11:23). Note the words *and does not doubt*. A spirit of certainty is absolutely essential for a successful World Prayer Missionary. The degree to which we are certain God is going to respond to our prayers will be the degree to which we will see that response become a reality.

Defining Our Focus

How do you determine your country, region, and base city as a World Prayer Missionary? The steps are simple:

First, *establish a systematic prayer strategy*. Set aside time over the next several days to pray about which region God wants you to target in your prayers. You may wish to use a book such as *Operation World*, Patrick Johnstone, STL Books, William Carey Library, or the *World Prayer Map*, Every Home for Christ, P.O. Box 7139, Canoga Park, CA 91304–7139.

Second, *pray systematically for several nations to help you select your country*. If you use the World Prayer Map, you will note the map is divided into 31 groups of seven countries. This allows you to pray for the entire world each month. You may wish to devote an entire month to the process of selecting a country. As you pray daily, note any countries to which you feel drawn for more concentrated prayer. Be especially sensitive to countries under Communist or Muslem dominance.

Third, *prayerfully narrow your focus to cover a region rather than the whole country*.

China provides a good example. This vast land is populated with more than a billion people. Focusing on all of China might be too general. Thus, the World Prayer Missionary might pray daily for one of China's almost thirty provinces and autonomous regions. The same would apply for the Soviet Union with fifteen republics, or India with twenty-two states. As the army of World Prayer Missionaries increases, all provinces and regions of the world will be covered.

Fourth, *search out specific information you can use as prayer fuel for your region of focus*. *Operation World* is an excellent source to help get you started. If, for example, you were to select the closed Communist country of Albania, you might list on 3 x 5 cards these facts for later use in your daily prayer strategy: Albania has a population of 3,000,000. The capital city is Tirana, with a population of 175,000 souls. Albania's specific peoples: Albanians (95%), Greeks (2.5%), and gypsies (2.4%). Albania is Europe's poorest and least-developed country. Its government is considered one of Europe's most ruthless Communist regimes. Albania's government leaders boast that their nation is the first officially atheistic state in the world. Atheism is the official state religion of Albania.

Number each of your facts because it is from this list that you will later compile a seven-day prayer strategy.

Fifth, *take a strategy development trip to your public library.* A visit to the library will greatly assist you in planning your strategy. Upon arrival ask the librarian where the encyclopedias and world atlases are found. If permitted, make a photocopy of the best map you can find of your country. Read the main article about your country in an encyclopedia such as *World Book.* As you work, begin translating simple facts about a nation and its peoples into potential prayer requests.

Take, for example, the Kwangtung province in southern China with a population exceeding 50 million. There are at least twenty large cities in the province, with Canton serving as its capital. All of these cities should be on your list. Later, when you implement them into your seven-day prayer strategy, you might list several of these cities for each day, thus allowing you to pray for all the main cities of that province each week. Remember, a missionary planning to go to a region would need to study cities targeted for ministry. As committed World Prayer Missionaries we need to take our calling just as seriously.

You'll also want to determine your base city as a World

Prayer Missionary. Generally, this will be the capital city of the nation or province.

When reading the primary article about your country, be sure to note the listing of other articles in that encyclopedia related to that same theme.

Sixth, *develop a spiritual warfare strategy for your region of focus.* After you have gleaned some basic information concerning your country, use it as the basis for developing a seven-day prayer strategy.

To accomplish this, you'll need to prepare "Prayer Warfare Strategy Cards" for each day of the week. Eventually you may have as many as two or even three cards for each day.

Next, divide all your facts into seven groups. From these lists you will develop a seven-day prayer strategy for your nation.

On one side of each card, note the day of the week and list that day's prayer facts. Certain facts you will want to include each day are your base city and other general prayer targets, like the overall population of the country. Then for each day in the week write the names of several cities that will be your intercessory targets. If you're praying for a larger country like China or India, and you do not feel directed to focus on just one province, divide the provinces up, praying for several each day so that once a week you have included all by name. The goal is to include enough in prayer each day to cover all your regions every seven days.

To give a hypothetical example, if your master list of general facts about your country includes twenty-eight focuses, and if, in addition, there are twenty-one main cities, you would pray for four different fact-focuses and three different cities (in addition to your base city) each day. In total you would have eight separate prayer opportunities per day.

On the opposite side of each 3 x 5 card you might wish to print several key verses of Scripture that you can use to keep the power of God's Word in your praying. List your favorite verses, plus some of the many positive verses recorded in this book.

Some sample verses might include Jeremiah 51:20, Isaiah 41:15, Jeremiah 1:10, 1 John 4:4, Matthew 28:18, Matthew 19:26, Luke 9:1–2, Luke 10:19, Micah 3:8, Mark 11:23, and Matthew 16:19.

Elsewhere on these cards you might want to include some of the suggestions for prayer as shared in our weekly guide to intercession presented earlier in this book.

Seventh, *develop your prayer mission both within and without your prayer closet.* Jesus said, "Men ought always to pray and not to faint" (Luke 18:1, KJV); and Paul wrote, "Pray without ceasing" (1 Thessalonians 5:17). This is the spirit of the World Prayer Missionary. We should take our prayer burden with us wherever we can. When a missionary goes to a land, he or she is consumed with that culture. No matter what that worker does, or where he goes in that land, he is still a missionary.

The World Prayer Missionary must cultivate this same quality. Our country of focus ought to go with us wherever we go. It's easy to tuck the cards with a day's strategy into pocket or purse to be prayed over whenever there's a pause in the day. And always remember, as a World Prayer Missionary you may be a housewife, schoolteacher, car salesman, or carpenter—but your real calling is a mission of prayer. You may go physically to a place of employment, but your heart is going to Europe, Asia, or Africa.

Ultimate Victory

Several weeks after the World Prayer Missionary concept was first introduced through our ministry, we began
to receive scores of commitment cards from intercessors
indicating they wished to enlist. On each card the intercessor noted the country he or she had selected for daily
prayer.

As the cards began to arrive I decided it would be good
to have special prayer over these firstfruits of a program I
believed would greatly honor the Lord in the future.

It happened to be our usual monthly day of prayer and
several of our regular intercessors had gathered, along
with a new, older brother I had not met before. He
introduced himself as Armando, and I recognized an
accent that originated somewhere in Europe. Later I
learned Armando was born near the Albanian border.

God had sent Armando that day to deliver an important
message.

We gathered in our small prayer chapel and after a
season of worship began to pray over the numerous
World Prayer Missionary commitment cards. The lights
were turned out in the prayer room except for a lighted
globe of the earth near the center of the small room. It
served as a special focus for what was about to happen.

As each warrior took a handful of cards we began to
pray, one at a time. We held the cards before the Lord,
thanking Him for these pioneer prayer missionaries. They
were the first of what I believed would become a vast army
of committed intercessors. They would be, I believed, an
army that would ultimately bind or restrain satanic power
over every geographic region on earth. At one point in our

prayer I expressed these feelings with the remark, "Wouldn't it be beautiful if an army of intercessors would someday rise up and restrain all demonic activity, confronting *every* demon at the same time throughout the world?"

I thought little of the theological implications of that remark until it was Armando's time to pray. Even the flavor of the brother's accent added something of significance to what God was about to say.

Armando began to pray a simple prayer of God's blessing on all these who were enlisting in the new army. Then he paused, and the look on his face was one of wonder. He began to nod his head, as tears ran down his face. He clutched his handful of commitment cards more tightly and lifted them toward the globe, pointing with the cards.

"God . . . He just talk to my heart," Armando said. "He tell me I must tell you that as soon as you raise up an army that binds every demon on earth, His Kingdom shall come."

The authority with which my brother spoke was remarkable. His statement was so absolute that it took my breath away. I wondered if there was any clear biblical basis for making such a statement. After all, God's Word alone is the standard upon which we must base all perceived divine guidance.

A few days later I read John's description of a war to end all wars in the heavenlies (Revelation 12:7–11). There I found a unique confirmation of Armando's insight.

As described in Revelation, Michael, one of God's chief angelic officers, leads his angelic army against Satan's demonic forces and overcomes them. Satan's defeat is so final, he and his demonic hordes are forced forever from the heavenlies. Most noteworthy is the fact that although angelic forces defeat Satan, they do so because saints on earth are applying their weaponry—"the blood of the Lamb and the word of their testimony" (Revelation 12:11).

While meditating on these thoughts I read a footnote in the margin of my Bible. The commentary explained that something would happen in the future, a mysterious miracle in the heavenlies, that would render Satan incapable of functioning any longer with his demonic powers in that vast, invisible arena. The commentary suggested that no one could know for certain what the mystery would be, but somehow the application of the blood of the Lamb and the word of the saints' testimony would make it impossible for Satan to operate any longer in that unseen sphere.

Could it be that a great army of intercessors, highly trained and deeply committed, might be a part of the cleansing of the heavenlies in this final spiritual battle? Was this what Armando was sensing in his spirit?

The answer, of course, will be known only when the full record of history is written and we stand before God on the threshold of eternity.

We *can* know this. Our prayers not only make a difference; in God's eyes they *are* the difference. If one person's prayers can restrain a demonic spirit, a thousand intercessors focusing their prayers on specific regions of the world can restrain the demonic spirits that reign there.

Imagine what could happen if our prayer army increased until every demonic spirit over every geographic region of the world was restrained at the very same moment! As soon as every spirit is bound in prayer, which will permit the Gospel to be preached fully in all nations, His Kingdom will be established.

Perhaps this is what Jesus had in mind when He said, ". . . This gospel of the kingdom will be preached in all the world as a witness to all the nations, and then the end will come" (Matthew 24:14).

Dick Eastman is the international president of Every Home for Christ, a world evangelization ministry that assists churches throughout the world in systematic literature distribution to every home in a region. To date, Every Home Crusades have been conducted in more than 100 countries, where 1.6 billion gospel booklets have been distributed and more than 15 million decisions/response cards have been received in EHC's 55 worldwide offices. Dick is the author of several additional books on prayer, including the two best sellers, *The Hour That Changes the World* and *No Easy Road:* Inspirational Thoughts on Prayer.

For further information and especially for details on becoming a World Prayer Missionary with the ministry of Dick Eastman, write:

Every Home for Christ
P.O. Box 35930
Colorado Springs, CO 80935-3593